AAT

ACCESS AWARD IN BUSINESS SKILLS LEVEL 1

Workbook

2017 Edition

For assessments from January 2018

First edition 2017
ISBN 9781 5097 1513 8
British Library Cataloguing-in-Publication Data
A catalogue record for this book is available from the British Library

Published by
BPP Learning Media Ltd
BPP House
Aldine Place
London
W12 8AA

www.bpp.com/learningmedia

Printed in the United Kingdom

Your learning materials, published by BPP Learning Media Ltd, are printed on paper obtained from traceable sustainable sources.

The contents of this book are intended as a guide and not professional advice. Although every effort has been made to ensure that the contents of this book are correct at the time of going to press, BPP Learning Media makes no warranty that the information in this book is accurate or complete and accepts no liability for any loss or damage suffered by any person acting or refraining from acting as a result of the material in this book.

We are grateful to the AAT for permission to reproduce the sample assessment(s). The answers to the sample assessment(s) have been published by the AAT. All other answers have been prepared by BPP Learning Media Ltd.

A note about copyright

Dear Customer

What does the little © mean and why does it matter?

Your market-leading BPP books, course materials and e-learning materials do not write and update themselves. People write them on their own behalf or as employees of an organisation that invests in this activity. Copyright law protects their livelihoods. It does so by creating rights over the use of the content.

Breach of copyright is a form of theft – as well as being a criminal offence in some jurisdictions, it is potentially a serious breach of professional ethics.

With current technology, things might seem a bit hazy but, basically, without the express permission of BPP Learning Media:

- Photocopying our materials is a breach of copyright
- Scanning, ripcasting or conversion of our digital materials into different file formats, uploading them to Facebook or e-mailing them to your friends is a breach of copyright

You can, of course, sell your books, in the form in which you have bought them – once you have finished with them. (Is this fair to your fellow students? We update for a reason.) Please note the e-products are sold on a single user licence basis: we do not supply 'unlock' codes to people who have bought them secondhand.

And what about outside the UK? BPP Learning Media strives to make our materials available at prices students can afford by local printing arrangements, pricing policies and partnerships which are clearly listed on our website. A tiny minority ignore this and indulge in criminal activity by illegally photocopying our material or supporting organisations that do. If they act illegally and unethically in one area, can you really trust them?

Contents

How to use this Workbook

This Workbook for the Access Award in Business Skills Level 1 has been written specifically to ensure comprehensive yet concise coverage of the assessment criteria. It is fully up to date as at October 2017 and reflects both the AAT's study guide and the sample assessment provided by the AAT.

This Workbook contains odd-numbered chapters containing the learning you need to do to prepare yourself for the assessment, and even-numbered chapters giving you assessment practice in the form of assessment style tasks.

You should work through the book taking each chapter in turn, working through the information presented to you and then attempting the tasks given. You can compare your answers with the answers given towards the back of the Workbook. If you have struggled with any tasks, look back at the learning chapter to see where you have gone wrong. At the end of the Workbook there is the sample assessment provided by the AAT plus two assessment-standard practice assessments prepared by BPP for you to work through. You should not attempt these until you have tried all the tasks in the even-numbered chapters. These sample and practice assessments have answers so that you can judge how you are doing once you have completed them.

If you have any comments about this book, please email nisarahmed@bpp.com or write to Nisar Ahmed, AAT Head of Programme, BPP Learning Media Ltd, BPP House, Aldine Place, London W12 8AA.

Learning outcomes

This assessment relates to three units.

Each of the units has a number of learning outcomes with assessment criteria in which students will need to demonstrate competence to complete this assessment.

Each chapter in this Workbook relates to the learning outcomes and assessment criteria below. Note that even-numbered chapters are assessment practice relating to the preceding chapter.

Preparing for work

The purpose of the unit

This unit will help students to prepare to seek employment in a wide range of sectors and to develop the skills that they need to contribute effectively in the workplace. Students will explore the key features of different types of organisations and the sectors in which they operate. They will learn the purpose of different organisations and how they operate, and also how organisations are commonly structured.

Learning objectives

On completion of this unit, students will understand the skills needed in the workplace, including the importance of team working, effective time management and the need for professional behaviour. They will explore workplace communications and the use of software for different business tasks, while understanding the need for data security and learning how to keep data secure. Finally, students will explore how to search for and identify a suitable job and then to complete a job application.

Learning outcomes

This unit consists of three learning outcomes, the student will:

1. Understand how organisations operate **[Chapter 1, sections 1 and 2]**
2. Develop skills for the workplace **[Chapter 1, section 2]**
3. Be able to apply or a job **[Chapter 1, section 3]**

Delivery guidance

Students must be able to complete tasks on the topics and procedures specified below.

Learning outcome 1 – Understand how organisations operate

Assessment criteria

1.1 Key features of different sectors **[Chapter 1, section 1]**

Students need to know:

- The key features of the retail sector:
  - Sells goods to the public
  - May have a number of branches, franchises or online
- The key features of the manufacturing sector:
  - Makes products either for sale or as components for further manufacturing
- The key features of the service sector:
  - Provides services rather than manufacturing or selling goods
- The key features of the charity sector:
  - Generates income to support its purpose
  - Governed by specific legislation
- The key features of the public sector:
  - Provides services to the public
  - Funded by government

1.2 Purpose of different types of organisation **[Chapter 1, section 1]**

Students need to know:

- That some organisations are run for profit:
  - Sole trader
  - Partnership
  - Private limited company
- That some organisations are not run for profit:
  - Charity
  - Public sector

1.3 Structure of an organisation **[Chapter 1, section 2]**

Students need to know:

- Typical departments within an organisation and what they do:
  - Production
  - Despatch
  - Finance
  - Sales and marketing
  - Information and communication technology (ICT)
  - Human resources

- The structure of a three-level organisation chart:
  - Directors
  - Department managers
  - Department staff
- Levels of responsibility in an organisation and who each level reports to (reporting lines):
  - Director
  - Manager
  - Staff

Learning outcome 2 – Develop skills for the workplace

Assessment criteria

2.1 Working with others **[Chapter 1, section 3]**

Students need to know:

- The characteristics of effective team working:
  - Leadership
  - Clear roles and responsibilities
  - Respect
  - Trust
  - Co-operation
  - Common goals
  - Realistic deadlines
  - Good communication
- The importance to a team of achieving goals:
  - Team morale
  - Success of the organisation

2.2 Time management **[Chapter 1, section 3]**

Students need to know:

- How to use planning aids to manage their time:
  - Calendars
  - Diaries
  - Work schedules
  - To-do lists
  - Checklists
- The effect on others of failing to meet a deadline:
  - Others may be relying on work produced by the team
  - Impact on other deadlines of the team
- That work might be allocated based on how urgent and important it is and who has asked for it to be carried out

Students must be able to:

- Plan allocated work based on time available

2.3 Professional behaviour **[Chapter 1, section 3]**

Students need to know:

- That they will be required to follow policies and procedures:
  - Use of social media
  - Use of personal phones
  - Dress codes
  - Answering business phone calls
- Principles of good time keeping:
- Being at work on time
  - Keeping to break times
  - Not leaving early
- Principles of polite communication with colleagues and customers:
  - Using correct names
  - Listening to the other person
  - Avoiding slang, swearing and offensive humour
  - Using 'please' and 'thank you'.

2.4 Workplace communications. **[Chapter 1, section 3]**

Students need to know:

- Methods of workplace communications:
  - Emails
  - Letters
  - Reports
  - Spreadsheets
  - Telephone calls
  - Face-to-face
  - Instant messaging
- Software for workplace communications:
  - Word processing
  - Spreadsheet
  - Email
  - Presentation

Students must be able to:

- Select appropriate method for workplace communications
- Select appropriate software for workplace communications

2.5 Understanding the importance of keeping data and information secure **[Chapter 1, section 3]**

Students need to know:

- Why it is important to make sure that data and information is secure:
  - Prevents loss and unauthorised sharing of information
  - Protects against computer failure or viruses
  - Maintains confidentiality
  - Protects customer information
  - Complies with any legal requirements
- How data and information is kept secure:
  - Passwords
  - Backups
  - Restricted access (both electronic and physical)
  - Anti-virus software

Students must be able to:

- Select a password that meets security requirements

Learning outcome 3 – Be able to apply for a job

Assessment criteria

3.1 Identifying a suitable job **[Chapter 1, section 4]**

Students need to know:

- Where to look for job vacancies:
  - Newspapers
  - Recruitment agencies
  - Job centre
  - Apprenticeship providers
  - Personal contacts
  - Recruitment websites
  - Social media
- How to identify requirements of job vacancies:
  - Skills
  - Personal qualities
  - Knowledge
  - Qualifications
  - Experience
  - Interests
- How to decide suitability for a job vacancy:
  - Essential requirements
  - Desirable requirements
  - Suitability of applicant for job vacancy based on requirements

3.2 Applying for a job using an application form or CV (*curriculum vitae*) **[Chapter 1, section 4]**

Students need to know:

- To include accurate personal details:
  - Current contact details
  - Job history
  - Qualifications
  - Relevant interests and experience
- The importance of:
  - Checking the application
  - Checking spelling
  - Having the application checked by someone else
  - Submitting the application by the closing date

Students must be able to:

- Complete an application for a job using an application form or CV

Using numbers in business

The purpose of the unit

Students will develop the skills to show that they can work effectively with numbers when applying for roles across a variety of areas within any business, including finance, customer services, administration and retail.

Learning objectives

On completion of this unit, students will have the skills to practically apply a range of common numerical methods to everyday business situations, whatever their role and regardless of the type of organisation in which they might work. They will be able to record and sort numbers, to identify differences between figures and to complete simple calculations. Students will be able to work out averages, use time and currency in calculations that support everyday business activities and work with more complex calculations, including those involving common decimals, fractions, percentages and proportions.

Learning outcome

This unit consists of three learning outcomes; the student will be able to:

1. Work with numbers **[Chapter 3, section 1]**
2. Perform simple business calculations **[Chapter 3, sections 1–3 and 10]**
3. Work with common decimals, fractions, percentages, proportions and ratios **[Chapter 3, sections 4–9]**

Delivery guidance

Students must be able to complete tasks on the topics and procedures specified below.

General

It is expected that students are able to use a standard calculator.

Learning outcome 1 – Working with numbers

Assessment criteria

1.1 Record and sort whole numbers **[Chapter 3, section 1]**

Students must be able to:

- Record numbers in words and figures
- Arrange numbers, including positive and negative numbers, in ascending and descending order
- Identify highest number
- Identify lowest number
- Calculate range
- Identify most frequently occurring number or numbers (mode)

Learning outcome 2 – Perform simple business calculations

Assessment criteria

2.1 Perform simple business calculations **[Chapter 3, section 1]**

Students need to know:

- How to use estimation/rounding
- How to estimate highest and lowest possible results
- How to use cross-checking

2.2 Identify differences between figures over time **[Chapter 3, section 1]**

Students must be able to:

- Identify increases
- Identify decreases

2.3 Complete calculations **[Chapter 3, sections 1–3 and 5)**

Students must be able to:

- Use numerical functions:
  - Addition
  - Subtraction
  - Multiplication
  - Division
  - Calculate average (mean)
- Work with common units of time:
  - Hours
  - Days
  - Weeks
  - Months
  - Quarters
  - Years
- Work with common units of currency

Learning outcome 3 – Work with common decimals, fractions, percentages, proportions and ratios

Assessment criteria

3.1 Calculate decimals, fractions and percentages of numbers **[Chapter 3, sections 6–8]**

Students must be able to:

- Calculate decimals
- Calculate simple fractions:
  - $\frac{1}{2}$
  - $\frac{1}{4}$
  - $\frac{1}{5}$
  - $\frac{1}{10}$
- Calculate whole percentages
- Calculate figures using whole percentages
- Express a number as a fraction or percentage of another

3.2 Calculate equivalent fractions, percentages and decimals **[Chapter 3, section 9]**

Students must be able to:

- Convert fractions into percentages and decimals
- Convert percentages into fractions and decimals
- Convert decimals into percentages and fractions

3.3 Calculate and apply simple proportions and ratios **[Chapter 3, section 4]**

Students must be able to:

- Express one number as a proportion of another
- Express two numbers as a ratio
- Apply a proportion or ratio to a number

3.4 Round numbers **[Chapter 3, section 1]**

Students must be able to:

- Round results of calculations to whole numbers
- Round results of calculations to two decimal places

Sales and purchases in business

The purpose of the unit

This unit focuses on organisations that aim to make a profit rather than those operating in the not-for-profit or public sector. Studying this unit will help students to understand the importance of sales and purchases, and the procedures that support them, to the success of those businesses.

On completion of this unit, students will understand that businesses make money by selling goods and services. Students will also understand that businesses have to use their income to pay for the costs of running the business. They will know the processes involved in making both sales and purchases and will understand how they can contribute to the success of a business by following business procedures accurately and on time.

Learning objectives

On completion of this unit, students will understand that businesses make money by selling goods and services. Students will also understand that businesses have to use their income to pay for the costs of running the business. They will know the processes involved in making both sales and purchases and will understand how they can contribute to the success of a business by following business procedures accurately and on time.

Learning outcomes

This unit consists of three learning outcomes, the student will:

1. Understand how sales and purchases support businesses **[Chapter 5, sections 1 and 2]**
2. Understand priniciples of sales and purchases **[Chapter 5, sections 3–5]**
3. Apply business procedures to sales and purchases **[Chapter 5, sections 3 and 6]**

Delivery guidance

Students must be able to complete tasks on the topics and procedures specified below.

Learning outcome 1 – Understand how sales and purchases support businesses

Assessment criteria

1.1 Sales and purchases in business **[Chapter 5, section 1]**

Students need to know:

- The importance of sales and purchases:
  - Businesses need money to operate
  - Selling goods and services makes money (income)
  - Buying goods and services costs money (expenses)
  - Businesses need more income than expenses to run profitably
  - The meaning of profit and loss: income minus expenses
- Possible problems when there is more expenditure than income:
  - Not enough money to pay for purchases
  - Bank account may become overdrawn
  - Suppliers may withdraw credit
  - Business could fail
- Possible opportunities when there is more income than expenditure:
  - Saving opportunity
  - Business growth

Learning outcome 2 – Understand priniciples of sales and purchases

Assessment criteria

2.1 Sales **[Chapter 5, section 2]**

Students need to know:

- Who goods or services are sold to:
  - Customers
  - Clients
- That some sales are made on a cash basis (income is received at the same time as the sale of goods or services)
- That some sales are made on a credit basis (income is received in an agreed period of time after the sale of goods or services)

2.2 Purchases **[Chapter 5, section 2]**

Students need to know:

- Who goods or services are bought from: suppliers
- That some purchases are made on a cash basis (payment is made at time of receiving goods or services)
- That some purchases are made on a credit basis (payment is made in an agreed period of time after receiving goods or services)
- That businesses may have a list of approved suppliers

2.3 Payment terms **[Chapter 5, section 2]**

Students need to know:

- The purpose of payment terms:
  - To ensure that customers know when to pay their invoices
  - To ensure that suppliers are paid at the agreed time
- Common terminology:
  - Payment in advance
  - Payment on delivery
  - Payment 10, 14, 30 or 60 days after invoice date
  - Payment at end of the month of invoice
- How payment terms offered to customers/clients and received from suppliers affect the bank balance

Learning outcome 3 – Apply business procedures to sales and purchases

Assessment criteria

3.1 Business procedures for sales and purchases **[Chapter 5, section 3]**

Students need to know:

- Why it is important to follow business procedures:
  - To avoid errors
  - To avoid missing internal and external deadlines
  - To ensure processes are completed as required by the business
  - To maintain good business relationships with customers and suppliers
- How to follow procedures:
  - Completing documents fully and accurately
  - Completing documents on time
  - Obtaining authorisation
- Documents used in the sales process:
  - Customer order
  - Delivery note
  - Sales invoice
- Documents used in the purchase process:
  - Approved supplier list
  - Purchase order
  - Delivery note
  - Goods received note (GRN)
  - Purchase invoice
- The process of making sales:
  - Customer places order
  - Business delivers goods or provides services to customer
  - Business invoices for goods or services
  - Business receives and records the income
- The process of purchasing goods or services:
  - Business selects supplier
  - Business raises purchase order
  - Business receives goods or services from supplier
  - Business checks delivery note against goods received
  - Business completes goods received note (GRN)
  - Business makes a note of any differences and queries them with supplier
  - Business checks purchase invoice against purchase order and delivery note/ goods received note (GRN)
  - Business makes payment and records the expenditure

Students must be able to:

- Complete documents used in the sales process (delivery note, sales invoice) with:
  - Date
  - Purchase order number
  - Delivery note number
  - Customer name and address
  - Description and quantity of goods or services
  - Value of goods or services including item price
  - Amounts (net, VAT and total)
- Select an approved supplier for specified goods or services
- Complete documents used in the purchase process (purchase order, goods received note (GRN)) with:
  - Date
  - Purchase order number
  - Supplier name and address
  - Description and quantity of goods or services
  - Value of goods or services including item price
  - Amounts (net, VAT and total)
- Check for differences between documents in the purchase process (purchase order, goods received note (GRN), delivery note):
  - Incorrect items or quantity of goods
  - Items missing from delivery
  - Incorrect item price
  - Incorrect calculations

Test specification

AAT Access Award in Business Skills – Level 1

Duration One and a half hours

Form of testing

Computer based assessment, marked by computer.

Assessment weighting

Learning outcomes	Weighting
Preparing for Work	
1. Understand how organisations operate	10%
2. Develop skills for the workplace	10%
3. Be able to apply for a job	10%
Using Numbers in Business	
1. Work with numbers	5%
2. Perform simple business calculations	10%
3. Work with common decimals, fractions, percentages, proportions and ratios	15%
Sales and Purchases in Business	
1. Understand how sales and purchases support businesses	5%
2. Understand principles of sales and purchases	10%
3. Apply business procedures to sales and purchases	15%
Integration	10%
Total	**100%**

1 Preparing for work

Chapter coverage

This chapter introduces the types of organisations you may encounter and describes the way that they are typically structured. It also covers skills that are required to be effective in the workplace and provides information about how to identify and apply for suitable job opportunities.

1 Types of organisation

Organisations may have a number of different purposes.

Commercial organisations aim to make a profit, usually by selling goods or providing services and are often referred to as businesses.

You may come across other types of organisation that do not seek to make a profit. These include government bodies whose purpose is to maximise service delivery to the public.

We can categorise an organisation by whether it is run for profit or not run for profit.

Organisations run for profit

This type of organisation, referred to as businesses, can take a number of forms dependent upon their ownership structure. The simplest form is a sole trader.

A **sole trader** is a business owned and run by an individual and there is no legal distinction between the business and the individual. Small service businesses, such as plumbers and electricians are often sole traders.

Partnerships are businesses owned and run by a number of individuals. Professional firms such as lawyers or accountants are often formed as partnerships. There are a number of different organisation types within each category as shown below. As with sole traders, there is no legal distinction between a partnership and the partners who own it.

A **limited company** is a separate legal entity from those who own it. Limited companies are owned by the shareholders who are not necessarily involved in running it. Shareholders appoint the board of directors who run the company.

How it works

The table below shows the different types of organisation that are run for profit:

Sole traders	Owned and run by an individual
Partnerships	Owned and run by a number of individuals
Limited companies	Owned by shareholders, run by directors

KEYWORDS

A **sole trader** is a small business run and owned by an individual

A **partnership** is a business owned and run by a number of individuals

A **limited company** is owned by shareholders and run by directors. Some companies are very large.

Organisations not run for profit

There are also organisations with different aims. These fall into two main categories.

Public sector organisations are funded by government and their aim is typically to maximise service delivery to the public or achieve an objective of government such as collecting taxes. Examples of public sector bodies include the Crown Prosecution Service, HM Revenue and Customs and the National Health Service (NHS).

Charities aim to raise money from the public which they spend in order to further their specified purpose. Some of the largest charities in the UK are Oxfam, the Arts Council of England and Cancer Research UK. Charities must be run in accordance with specific charities legislation.

How it works

The table below shows the different types of organisation that are not run for profit:

Public sector	Government funded	Service delivery to the public or achieve government objective
Charities	Funded by the public	Support specified purpose

KEYWORDS

Organisations in the **public sector** are funded by governments to deliver services or achieve government aims.

Charities raise money in order to spend it on a specified purpose.

TASK 1 **Fill in the gaps in the sentences below, using words given in the options. You may have to use the same word more than once.**

Limited companies aim to make a ______.

The National Health Service does not exist to make a ______.

Options:

cost saving
profit

Sectors

We can also categorise organisations by sector. This looks at the nature of the organisation's main activities. We have just looked at two of these: charities and the public sector. Organisations run for profit (ie businesses) can be involved in a range of commercial activities.

How it works

The table below shows the different sectors organisations may fall into:

Sector	Features	Examples
Retail	Sell goods to the public May operate through physical branches or franchises May also operate online	Tesco Amazon Gap
Manufacturing	Produce finished goods or components for further manufacturing	Rolls Royce Unilever
Services	Provide services Customers may be the public or other organisations	HSBC Aviva
Public sector	Service delivery to the public or achieve government objective	Police service BBC NHS
Charities	Support specified purpose	Oxfam Save the Children

At this stage of your studies, you do not need to know anything more about these types of organisation, only the sectors they are in and the main purpose of organisations in those sectors.

TASK 2 Sector classification

For each of the following businesses, select the sector that they operate in.

A travel agent

A maker of musical instruments

An online bookseller

Options:

Manufacturing
Public sector
Retail
Services

2 Organisational structure

A sole trader such as an electrician may just be one person without any employees. That person will provide the service as an electrician, but on top of this will have to do many other tasks associated with a business, such as answer the phone, prepare and send out quotations, prepare and send invoices, maintain accounting records, organise advertising etc.

As organisations get larger they are typically split into departments, each handling a different part of the organisation's workload. This approach allows staff members to specialise in particular tasks for increased efficiency.

Departmental structure

The table below describes typical departments in an organisation and what they do.

Department	Responsibilities
Production	Ensuring that raw materials are made into finished goods efficiently
Despatch	Getting goods to the customer, including packaging and delivery
Finance	The capture and use of financial information, including the preparation of accounting information
Sales and marketing	Advertising, promotion and public relations, together with interactions with customers
Information and communication technology (ICT)	Operating and supporting ICT systems and ensuring that they assist an organisation in meeting its objectives
Human resources	Managing an organisation's staff including recruitment, legal compliance, training and compensation

The size of each department will be affected by the size of the organisation. For example, the finance department of a small sole trader may just be a single accountant, whereas a very large company might employ several hundred people in this department. It will also be related to the sector in which it operates. For example a service sector organisation such as a partnership of lawyer would not need a production department.

Some departments such as despatch and sales and marketing are focused on servicing customer needs, whereas others, such as human resources and ICT, are more internal focussed and meet the needs of other departments.

TASK 3 Which departments would be responsible for the following tasks at an organisation?

Making sure factory machinery is maintained	
Producing an employment contract for new staff	
Producing budgets for management	

Options:

Finance
Human resources
Information and communication technology
Production

Organisational reporting lines

As organisations get larger it is important that they are well organised. It is essential that all employees know what their role is and who they report to.

The structure of who members of staff report to is referred to as an organisation's reporting lines. If you report to someone they are responsible for setting your objectives and goals and evaluating your performance. They are also the primary person to whom you should raise issues related to your employment functions.

How it works

Those working in an organisation can be put into three levels.

	Responsibility	Reports to
Directors	Formulating business objectives and strategy to achieve them	Shareholders (owners)
Managers	Day-to-day management consistent with strategy and objectives	Director responsible for that department
Staff	Performing departmental function assigned to them	Department manager

Reporting lines in a large organisation are usually based on departments. For example, a bookkeeper working in the finance department would report to the finance manager, who would in turn report to the organisation's finance director.

In a really large organisation there could be many other stages in reporting lines such as junior managers reporting to senior managers.

The structure of an organisation can be thought of as a pyramid with more individuals making up each level as you go down.

KEYWORD

Reporting lines describe the organisational structure determining who is responsible for setting goals and evaluating performance of each staff member.

3 Developing workplace skills

It is important to develop appropriate skills to be effective in the workplace. Some roles have specific technical skill requirements, for instance to work in a finance department you would be likely to need some accounting skills; similarly, to work in the ICT department you would need specific IT skills. However, your assessment is concerned with the many workplace skills that are relevant to all those working in an organisation.

Working with others

Nearly all roles that an employee could fill at an organisation involve some degree of interaction with other employees and third parties such as customers and suppliers.

There are a number of workplace practices and behaviours that, if adopted by employees, are likely to lead to greater organisational efficiency. In addition they are likely to lead to an individual being more successful in their job.

Working effectively with others is particularly important when employees work in teams. If a team works more effectively it is more likely to achieve the goals set for it. This is likely to lead to:

- **Better team morale**: If goals are achieved or exceeded all members of the team are likely to feel a sense of shared success and be more motivated in future. If the team fails to meet goals its members are likely to less motivated, may feel a sense of failure and may look to blame individual team members.
- **Success of the organisation**: Properly set team goals should be designed to assist in achieving organisational goals. Therefore if individual team goals are met the organisation is more likely to reach its objectives.

How it works

Effective team working involves the following characteristics:

Characteristic	Explanation
Leadership	All teams need a leader, but not all team members can be involved in leadership. Any effective team should have a nominated team leader. Leadership requires a number of skills including organisation, communication and the ability to motivate.
Clear roles and responsibilities	The team leader is responsible for clearly communicating to each team member their role and objectives. If this is not done, work may be duplicated or omitted.
Respect	Members of a team will have different strengths and weaknesses. Each member of the team should be given tasks appropriate to their skills. The way team members interact with each other should be respectful and recognise each person's contribution.
Trust	Team members are dependent on each other in achieving goals. Therefore they need to feel that they can rely on each other. Behaviour such as seeking to blame other team members for problems or not working as hard as other team members can undermine trust.

Characteristic	Explanation
Co-operation	A team member experiencing problems should be given assistance, not simply criticised. If a team member has finished an assigned task, they should seek to assist a team member falling behind, not take a rest.
Common goals	As well as having a clear understanding of their own role, team members need a shared understanding of their common goal.
Realistic deadlines	When a team leader sets goals it is important that these are not unrealistic. Being asked to perform a task that cannot be done in the time allotted will be very demotivating.
Good communication skills	Communication should be two way. The team leader needs to communicate goals. Team members need to provide feedback to the leader and ask for help if additional information or resources are required.

TASK 4 **Indicate which of the following is an example of behaviour consistent with effective team working:**

(i) Telling a team member who is falling behind that they are useless and letting the team down

(ii) The team leader asking team members to sort out who will perform each task amongst themselves

(iii) Working extremely hard so that you are able to finish your task and leave work early that day

(iv) Informing the team leader that you have found the task assigned to you difficult and that you are falling behind schedule

Time management

At its simplest, time management means using the available time at work to achieve as much as possible. This involves using time efficiently by prioritising tasks effectively.

As an employee you have limited time to accomplish the objectives set. Therefore it is important to get the most from the scarce resource of time. If employees waste time they are likely to be less successful in achieving their personal goals and in assisting the organisation to meet its objectives.

Poor time management doesn't only adversely affect the individual employee. It can also have implications for:

- The individual's team: A team can be let down by the failure of one of its members to meet a deadline.
- Other employees who depend on the individual's work: For example, a production process may consist of a number of processes performed in sequence. If, due to poor time management, one employee fails to complete the part of the process for which they are responsible on time, other employees later in the production process may also be unable to meet their targets.

How it works

For example, if the sales clerk does not process invoices, the credit controller will not have an up-to-date record of who owes money, and when it's due. As another example, if a purchases clerk does not process invoices, the payments clerk does not know who to pay, or when.

This is another reason why communication is vital: if one person is going to miss a deadline, it may mean that everyone in the team goes on to miss their own deadlines, and the work of the whole function becomes inefficient.

Time management tools

Planning is an important aspect of time management. There are a number of planning aids that can be used to assist in effective time management.

Tool	Description
Diaries	A workplace diary is used to record things that you need to do such as appointments, meetings and task deadlines. Because it is organised by date, it makes it easy to quickly see what commitments you have on a given day. Traditionally diaries were books in which you wrote the details, whereas today it is more likely to be software on your computer or phone.
Calendars	In the past, a calendar was something you hung on the wall, or kept on a desk which showed the dates of the month whereas a diary was a book. With the move of such tools onto your computer or phone the distinction between diary and calendar has become blurred and the words have become largely interchangeable. For example 'Calendar' in Microsoft Outlook performs the functions of what would have been traditionally be described as a diary.

Tool	Description
Work schedule	A work schedule also records outstanding tasks. However, it is slightly different to a calendar/diary as it will contain not just task deadlines, but also allocate available time to each task. So a work schedule shows when work is scheduled to be done, not just when it must be done by. This helps to allocate your time to tasks.
To-do lists	A to-do list records outstanding things that you have to do. This might include phone calls, meetings, outstanding tasks etc. A to-do list is a valuable tool for ensuring you don't forget to do something when you are busy. To-do lists may be maintained on paper or on your computer.
Checklists	Checklists are also a tool to avoid forgetting a task. Checklists are a list of standard procedures or tasks that need to be performed. As these tasks are performed they are 'ticked off' to ensure that none are omitted. For example, the end of each month is usually a busy time for an organisation's accounts department and a month-end checklist could be used to make sure nothing is overlooked.

All the tools above assist effective time management by recording things that an employee has to do. Knowing what you have to do is an important first stage, but you then need to apply another key skill by prioritising these tasks appropriately.

Prioritisation involves a consideration of the importance of a task and whether the performance of other tasks by that employee or others depends on its completion. In prioritising a task it will also be necessary to estimate how long each task is likely to take.

TASK 5 Prioritisation

Today is 14 September and you have three tasks on your to-do list.

Task	Description	Completion required by
A	Get filing up to date	15 September
B	Prepare estimates of raw materials required in October to purchasing department	15 September
C	Calculate material usage for the month and provide to accounts	30 September

You enjoy calculating material usage for task C, however you find preparing estimates for Task B more difficult and have been putting it off. Task A, getting your filing up to date, is something you always aim do by the middle of the month and you include it on your to do list to prevent your filing getting out of control.

What order should you perform these tasks in?

Professional behaviour

As an employee you will be expected to conduct yourself in a professional manner consistent with your role.

Some aspects of what is expected of you will be set out in writing by your employer in employment policies or procedures. These could be included in your employment contract, but are more likely to be contained in a procedures manual, employee handbook or similar.

How it works

The following are examples of issues covered by an employer's procedures and policies:

Issue	Explanation
Use of personal phones	If an employee spends time on a personal phone this reduces their effectiveness and may also disturb others. Therefore a policy may state that personal phone usage should be kept to a minimum.
Use of social media	Use of social media either via a personal phone or an office computer whilst at work also reduces an employee's effectiveness. Company policy is likely to prohibit use of social media at work. Additionally it may specify that employees should not make social media posts related to their work activities even when using social media out of work as this may breach confidentiality.
Dress code	Many roles will have guidelines regarding what an employee wears. For example, if a role involves dealing face-to-face with customers, employees are likely to be required to be smart and neat in their appearance. Some employees may be required to wear a uniform. Other more detailed policies may cover areas such as jewellery or hairstyle. This could be safety related such as a prohibition on long loose hair or long earrings in a factory environment with machinery.
Answering the phone	Many employees may be responsible for answering business phone calls such as those from customers or suppliers. Some companies have detailed procedures regarding phone interactions to ensure that employees greet customers/suppliers appropriately, provide all necessary information and collect information needed by the business.

Another important aspect of professional behaviour is good time keeping. An employee who is continually late or fails to make appointments reduces not just their own efficiency, but also that of others.

Good time keeping encompasses the following:

- Arriving at work on time
- Not leaving early
- Keeping to specified break times
- Arriving promptly to meetings and appointments

In addition to reducing your own efficiency, arriving late is discourteous to those you have kept waiting.

There are other aspects of politeness that are part of the standards of professional behaviour expected of employees. These include:

Using correct names: Calling a co-worker by a nickname or a contraction of their full name is not appropriate unless it has been made clear that it is how they wish to be addressed. For example if a co-worker is called Mohan do not address them as 'Mo' unless they have told you that is how they wish to be addressed.

Avoiding slang and swearing: Co-workers and others you come into contact with may be offended by swearing and slang. Remember just because you would not be offended doesn't mean others aren't.

Avoiding offensive humour: Telling a joke may offend those who are the butt of the joke, it could also have a theme that some find offensive. Humour is a very difficult area to get right in a diverse workplace, as what one individual finds amusing may highly offend another person. Good advice in relation to jokes might be 'if in doubt don't tell it'.

Listening to other people: Virtually all job roles involve meetings and discussions with other people. Remember that these interactions should be two way, listening to others is as important as speaking. Speaking over other people is clearly impolite, but it is also important to make it clear that you are listening to what others say.

Basic courtesy: This is important regardless of how busy you are. Saying 'please' and 'thank you' takes no time and failure to do so may be perceived as a deliberate sleight. The use of polite courtesy is expected in personal interactions, both verbal and in writing.

Workplace communication

Fifty years ago there were only three main forms of communication: face-to-face; telephone or in writing. In the world of today there are now many other forms of electronic communication that may be used in the workplace.

How it works

The following are examples of types of workplace communication:

Communication	Explanation
Face-to-face	Although it may be more time consuming, face-to-face communication can have advantages. Non-verbal communication can reduce the potential for misunderstandings. Something as simple as knowing whether someone is smiling, may affect your understanding of how serious a comment is.
Telephone	Although you can't see the person you can still hear 'how' something is said. This still reduces the potential for misunderstanding. However, a phone call is not possible if the person isn't free to take the call. Like face-to-face communication, it requires both parties to be simultaneously available.
Letter	Letters lack the immediacy of direct communication. They are also slow as the letter has to reach the intended recipient before it can be read. However, there is the advantage that a letter is permanent and is useful for setting out complex matters clearly. Also a letter is seen as more formal and might be used for a situation such as making a complaint.
Email	Email has the advantage over a letter of immediate delivery to the recipient (although they still have to open and read it). By convention emails tend to be written in a less formal style that a traditional letter.
Instant messaging	This real-time text-based direct communication method is more immediate than email. This might be used internally in an organisation as a short request for information. It is often used with customers as a way of offering online website help. The style of communication tends to be even less formal than email and is most suited to short messages.
Reports	These are a standardised way of presenting information. An example might be a monthly sales report that you send to the sales manager. This may well be an electronic rather than a physical document that you attach to an email. Reports are a way of presenting information rather than just a communication method.
Spreadsheets	If you wish to present numerical information this may be done using a spreadsheet. A spreadsheet is just an digital table of numbers. If you send a monthly sales report to the sales manager it may well contain a spreadsheet, perhaps breaking down sales at each branch per week.

Within the work environment there are a number of software applications that may be used to assist with communications. These incude:

- **Spreadsheet software**: Used to create, view and amend spreadsheets
- **Word processing software**: Used to create documents such as letters and reports. These may be physically printed and sent to a recipient or attached to an email in electronic form.
- **Presentation software**: Allows the user to create slides that make up a presentation. Such presentations may be sent to a recipient to view (electronically or physically), or may be used to support a presentation that an individual delivers.
- **Email software**: Used both for the creation and sending of emails, and to view, store and manage emails that are received.

In your assessment, questions may require you to select the most appropriate method for a given workplace communication. You may also need to know which type of software would be used to support a given workplace communication.

TASK 6 Using an appropriate communication method

Select the most appropriate method of communication in each of the situations in the finance department below.

Notifying a customer who has failed to pay an invoice that you intend to take legal action.	
Asking the sales department for the total of last week's sales.	
Discussing job performance with an employee.	

Options:

Email
Face-to-face
Letter
Report

Information security

In the workplace is very often sensitive; the organisation could be harmed if it became public. The organisation need to keep that information private, in other words secret, within the organisation. Another word for this privacy is **confidentiality**.

KEYWORD

Confidentiality is the concept of keeping sensitive information private.

Why might a business want to keep information confidential?

Customers might not be happy at the amount of profit that the organisation makes on sales to them, and buy from someone else...

Suppliers might not be happy at the amount of profit that the organisation makes on items that the suppliers sell to the organisation, so they may raise their prices, or attempt to cut out the organisation and sell direct to its customers...

If sensitive information becomes public knowledge, it can be very damaging to the organisation and even affect whether it can continue trading.

There is even information produced by an organisation that it might not want its own staff to know:

Future pay rises	Business plans involving redundancy	Business plans involving relocation

There are many other reasons, beyond simple confidentiality, for organisations to keep information and data secure. These include:

- **Avoiding loss**: The loss of valuable information could cause direct loss to an organisation – for example, if an organisation loses the information about which customers owe it money.
- **Avoiding computer failures and viruses**: A failure to keep data secure could give criminals access to an organisation's computer systems. This could allow the criminal to damage computer systems, for example by computer viruses.
- **Protecting customer information**: Even if loss of data does not affect a company directly, it could adversely affect its customers. This would be the case if customers' credit card details got into the hands of criminals.
- **Legal requirements**: The UK, like most countries, has specific laws placing specific responsibilities on how organisations hold and use personal data.

So, how does an organisation keep information and data secure?

How it works

The ways in which an organisation's data and information are kept secure include the following:

Passwords	Most information in an organisation is usually held in digital form in its IT system. Therefore it is important to control access to this system. If each staff member needs a password to access IT systems it can help to prevent unauthorised persons getting access. Effective passwords should be selected by employees that cannot easily be guessed. So passwords like 'password', 1234, your name or the company name should be avoided. The most effective passwords include letters and numbers as well as special characters such as '#' or '@'. A mixture of upper and lower case letters also makes a password more effective.
Back-ups	Regularly copying all data and storing it at another location enables an organisation to restore it in the event it is damaged or lost.
Access restrictions	As well as preventing unauthorised third parties from accessing data, passwords can also be used to control what parts of the system each employee has access to. Physical access controls are also important. For example, third parties should not be allowed into areas where confidential information is held such as private offices. Similarly, employees should take sensible steps such as keeping sensitive documents in a locked filing cabinet and not looking at sensitive information on a computer screen where it could be observed.
Anti-virus software	Dedicated software can be installed on computer systems to detect computer viruses that could damage systems and data. Once installed such systems automatically provide protection against viruses.

TASK 7 Effective passwords

Which of the following would be the most secure password for an employee called Amir Singh?

AmirS ☐

PASSWORD ☐

Computer ☐

@mirS1ngh23 ☐

4 Applying for a job

Applying for a job involves sending an application form or a document summarising your skills and experience. This is known as a CV (short for *curriculum vitae*) to the potential employer. Before this, you need to know where to find information about available jobs and how to identify which jobs are most suitable for you.

Identifying a suitable job

If you are looking for employment there are a number of places that you can search. These include:

- **Newspapers**: Employers may advertise positions available in newspapers and magazines. This method has reduced in its importance due to the development of the internet.
- **Recruitment websites**: These fulfil a similar role to adverts in newspapers. They have the advantage for employers that job ads can rapidly be posted and may also give the jobseeker useful facilities such as the ability to search and filter jobs by characteristics such as location and job description.
- **Recruitment agencies**: These are commercial organisations which are paid by employers to find candidates to fill vacancies. As a job seeker you would speak to an adviser who will try to match your skills and experience to an appropriate vacancy. The job seeker does not have to pay to use a recruitment agency.
- **Job centres**: The government funds job centres. They provide a similar service to recruitment centres by trying to match job seekers to available positions. It operates through physical branches as well as running a job search website.
- **Apprenticeship providers**: Employers may offer apprenticeships which combine working with studying to gain skills and knowledge in a specific job. Employers can receive government funding for the training element to encourage them to offer apprenticeships. The government offers an apprenticeship search facility online.
- **Social media**: Increasingly, employers are advertising job vacancies using social media such as Facebook or Twitter.

In addition to these resources, when looking for a job opportunity you should also ask your network of personal contacts if they are aware of any job opportunities. Individuals that you know may be aware that their employers have vacancies that they are looking to fill. Personal contacts may also recommend you which could give you an advantage.

Job requirements

Job adverts have a number of key features that will help you decide if that opportunity is appropriate for you.

How it works

An advert for a job vacancy may specify the following requirements:

Skills	Skills may be specified by employers. For example the ability to use spreadsheet or word processing software.
Personal qualities	All employers want staff to display general characteristics such as punctuality and politeness. For some positions there may be specific personal characteristic that are important. For example, for a sales role strong interpersonal skills are important, whereas for an accounts clerk accuracy and attention to detail may be seen as more important.
Knowledge	Some roles may also require knowledge. For example working as a clerk in an accounts department may require some knowledge of accounting practices.
Experience	In a way this is linked to knowledge and skills. Experience provides knowledge and skills and shows the potential employer that you can already perform the tasks involved in the role.
Qualifications	Possession of a qualification is another way of demonstrating to employers that you have a particular set of skills and knowledge.
Interests	Although not directly relevant to an advertised position, employers will still wish to know your interests. These may indicate your personal characteristics. For example, if you play a sport such as football you are probably likely to understand the importance of teamwork.

Job adverts may contain a number of the requirements above. These are usually broken down into essential requirements and desirable requirements.

To be considered by the employer for the position you **must** have essential requirements whereas possession of desirable requirements will give you an advantage over other applicants.

How it works

A job advert for a sales position might include the following requirements:

Essential requirements:

- Two years experience in a sales role
- Proficient in the use of word processing software
- Strong interpersonal skills
- Smart appearance

Desirable requirements:

- Fluency in a European language
- Familiarity with spreadsheet software

If you have six months' experience in sales but can speak French and Spanish fluently, you would not be eligible to be considered for this position as you lack an essential requirement.

If you have two years sales experience but only speak English, you are eligible to apply for the job, although candidates who can speak a European language will have an advantage over you.

To establish that a job opportunity is suitable you need to ensure that you satisfy all of the essential requirements. You should also consider the desirable requirements because the more of these you satisfy, the more likely your application is to be successful.

Job application forms and CVs

To apply for many jobs it will be necessary to complete an application form provided by the potential employer. The purpose of the application form is to collect information about your skills, experience and qualifications as well as obtaining basic personal information such as contact details. Considerable care should be taken in filling in a job application as it will be the first impression of you that a potential employer gets. A badly filled in application form with spelling mistakes and poor handwriting will not help you get a job.

Alternatively a job advert may ask you to send a CV (this is short for the Latin phrase *curriculum vitae*, but is rarely used in full). A CV provides the same sort of information as required to complete an application form. However, with a CV it is up to you exactly what information you present and how you organise and present it. This is important because a badly presented CV may harm your chances of getting the job.

Information typically included on an application form or CV includes:

- **Contact details**: Typically postal address, phone numbers and email.

- **Job history**: For each period of previous employment you should describe who you worked for, the period of employment, your job title and what the role involved.
- **Qualifications**: You should include any qualifications you received in full-time education and subsequently. You should specify the qualification, when it was achieved and the grade or mark achieved if relevant.
- **Relevant experience**: This overlaps with your job history and is an opportunity to highlight any experience gained that is relevant to the position you are applying for.
- **Interests**: You should describe your favourite pastimes and any achievements outside work. These are an indication to the employer of the sort of person you are.

You should take great care in preparing a job application or CV. First impressions are very important. An employer may get a very large number of applications from which they need to create a shortlist of candidates for interview. One way to do this is to exclude applicants who submit poorly completed applications or CVs.

KEYWORDS

A **CV (*curriculum vitae*)** is a document produced by a job applicant detailing skills, experience and qualifications and providing personal information such as contact details.

When completing the application or CV you should:

- **Check the application carefully yourself**: Ensure that the information is correct and complete. Is the use of English correct?
- **Check spelling**: If you complete documents using word processing software it is likely to include a spellcheck facility you can use.
- **Have another person check it**: It is hard to spot your own mistakes, so it is extremely useful to have another person check it. They may also be able to point out anything which is unclear.
- **Ensure you follow instructions**: This includes completing an application form correctly and submitting it to the right person at the correct address. It is also obviously important to submit your application before the specified closing date.

TASK 8 Completing an application form

Permanent Sales Consultant

The role involves selling financial products at face-to-face meetings. This will principally involve travelling to meet clients at their home or office at a time convenient to them.

The successful applicant must have excellent communication and selling skills and have at least two years sales experience. Knowledge of financial products or the ability to speak a second language would be an advantage.

The position carries a base salary plus a bonus based on the level of sales achieved.

Select three statements that would make an applicant suitable for this position.

I like to work in an office environment.	
I worked for three years as a purchase ledger clerk.	
I need a job with regular hours.	
I worked for three years selling mobile phone contracts.	
I have done a training course covering financial products.	
I speak three languages fluently.	

Chapter overview

There are many organisations that exist to make a profit, but there are also organisations with different aims such as the public sector and charities.

Businesses fall into different sectors such as services, retail and manufacturing.

All but the smallest organisations are organised into departments with specific responsibilities.

Organisations have reporting lines which determine who sets each employee's goals and evaluates their performance.

Effective employees need to develop a number of workplace skills.

Nearly all jobs involve some degree of working with others, which makes teamwork important.

Time is a scarce resource and it is important to adopt practices that lead to good time management.

All employees are expected to adhere to professional standards of behaviour such as having good timekeeping and communicating in a polite manner.

There are a number of procedures that an organisation can use to keep information and data secure, including passwords and physical access controls.

Communication skills are very important in the workplace. Part of this is knowing which communication methods are appropriate to a given situation.

Computer data and other information held by organisations may be sensitive and should be kept confidential.

Information and data is a valuable asset for organisations so its loss or destruction may be costly. There are many steps that can be taken to avoid this, such as installing anti-virus software on IT systems and using effective passwords.

To get a job you first need to identify an appropriate opportunity from the available sources of vacancies such as recruitment websites, job centres and newspapers.

Job vacancies specify the requirements for applicants. These may be essential or desirable.

Once a suitable job vacancy has been identified you need to either send your CV or request and fill in a job application form.

The way you fill out an application or produce your CV is the first impression that a potential employer gets of you.

Keywords

CHARITIES raise money in order to spend it on a specified purpose.

A **LIMITED COMPANY** is owned by shareholders and run by directors. Some companies are very large.

A **PARTNERSHIP** is a business owned and run by a number of individuals.

Organisations in the **PUBLIC SECTOR** are funded by government to deliver services or achieve government aims.

A **SOLE TRADER** is a small business run and owned by an individual.

CONFIDENTIALITY is the concept of keeping sensitive information private.

A **CV (CURRICULUM VITAE)** is a document produced by a job applicant detailing skills, experience and qualifications and providing personal information such as contact details.

2

Preparing for work: Test your learning

This chapter gives you question practice on the topics you covered in the previous chapter. The questions are in the same style you can expect in your assessment. You can find the answers at the back of this Workbook.

1 There are different types of organisation.

Complete the following sentences by selecting the most appropriate option from the list of items below each sentence.

(a) A sole trader is a [ ] organisation.

- private sector
- public sector
- charitable

(b) The police service [ ] aim to make a profit.

- does
- does not

2 It is important to understand the role of the finance department within an organisation.

Indicate whether the following statements are true or false.

(a) Detailed expenditure analysis provided by the finance department of a partnership is used by the general public to make business decisions.

True ☐

False ☐

(b) An organisation's ICT department provides a service to customers and suppliers.

True ☐

False ☐

3 It is important to observe confidentiality.

Complete the following sentences by inserting the most appropriate option from the list below each sentence.

Information about pay increases held on a computer should be kept

☐

- in an area to which all employees have access.
- in a password-protected file with access restricted to those who need the information.

A supplier of the organisation where you work asks you who the main customers of the organisation are. You reply:

☐

- 'I am sorry but I cannot give you any information, as it is confidential.'
- 'As you are a supplier I can tell you that it is Matlins and Swindells.'

4 Employees should behave in a professional manner.

Indicate whether the following statements are true or false.

Frequently arriving late for work is fine if it is because your train is late.

True ☐

False ☐

Use of personal phones at work is acceptable provided that you leave the office to avoid disturbing colleagues.

True ☐

False ☐

5 Methods of workplace communication

(a) **Complete this sentence by inserting the most appropriate option from the list below each box.**

Communicating by letter is [ ] for communications when [ ] is not of the highest importance.

- necessary
- appropriate
- inappropriate

- speed
- formality
- privacy

Working with others

(b) **Indicate whether the following statements are true or false.**

Teams work best when members are given clear goals by the team leader.

True ☐

False ☐

Giving team members unrealistic deadlines will ensure that they work harder.

True ☐

False ☐

6 Time management

(a) **Complete this sentence by inserting the most appropriate option from the list below each box.**

Tasks should be allocated to the time available based on their [ ] and their [ ].

- length
- urgency

- importance
- difficulty

(b) **Indicate whether the following statements are true or false.**

Diaries and calendars can be physical documents or computer software.

True ☐

False ☐

A calendar is the most appropriate tool for making sure that you do not forget to complete a task when you are busy.

True ☐

False ☐

7 Identifying a suitable job

The following job vacancy has been advertised by a local employer.

> **Position – Assistant to the financial controller**
>
> The successful applicant for this position must have strong organisational and communication skills and a high level of competence with both spreadsheet and word processing software.
>
> Previous experience of working in a finance department and basic knowledge of accounting are desirable.
>
> Please submit your CV by 30 May 20XX.

(a) **Which of the three individuals below is the most suitable applicant for the job?**

Rashida – She has worked for a year as an accounts clerk and has been on a number of training courses covering basic accounting. She can use spreadsheet software, but has never used word processing software.

Phillip – He has worked as a personal assistant to the production manager at a large manufacturer. The role involved extensive use of both spreadsheets and word processing software.

Françoise – She has just left college where she took a business studies course which included an accounting module. She is currently studying to improve her English skills.

☐

(b) The closing date for applications is tomorrow.

Given this, which of the following would be the best course of action?

☐ Quickly prepare your CV and send it by email today.

☐ Carefully prepare and check your CV and deliver it tomorrow by hand.

☐ Send an email asking for more time to complete a CV.

3 Using numbers in business

Chapter coverage

This chapter covers basic numeracy skills essential for the business environment. This includes recording, sorting and performing common calculations. Candidates need to be able to work with currency, units of time, decimals fractions and ratios. This chapter assumes that you will take a calculator to your assessment, which you are expected to do.

1 Numbers in business

Numbers are a key part of business and are commonly encountered as a monetary amount as well as being used to describe other business characteristics such as the quantity of goods sold.

Numbers can be recorded in figures or words. For example an organisation's current bank balance could be described as £3,451.34 or three thousand, four hundred and fifty one pounds and thirty four pence.

Ranking numbers

In your assessment you may be required to rank numbers in order of size. The order of ranking could be specified as ascending or descending size.

Let's consider an example:

The table below describes Jazz Co's bank balance at the end of each of the last four months.

January	February	March	April
£	£	£	£
1,209.89	980.42	4,654.68	3,452.34

You may need to rank these balances in **ascending order**. This would mean that you start with the smallest value.

Month	£
February	980.42
January	1,209.89
April	3,452.34
March	4,654.68

If you are asked to rank in **descending order** you would start with the largest number.

Month	£
March	4,654.68
April	3,452.34
January	1,209.89
February	980.42

So far the balance at the end of each month has been positive. You may also come across negative values and have to include these in a ranking.

Jazz Co's bank balance goes into overdraft (effectively a negative bank balance) for the next two months, so the month-end balances are as follows:

January	February	March	April	May	June
£	£	£	£	£	£
1,209.89	980.42	4,654.68	3,452.34	– 1,983.21	– 867.32

Negative numbers may also be shown as numbers in brackets. This is particularly common in accounting information.

January	February	March	April	May	June
£	£	£	£	£	£
1,209.89	980.42	4,654.68	3,452.34	(1,983.21)	(867.32)

One thing you need to be careful with when dealing with negative numbers is that a large negative number is a lower value. So Jazz's month-end balance in May is a lower than June. So if we rank the month-end values for all six months in ascending order we start with the lowest value, which is May:

Month	£
May	(1,983.21)
June	(867.32)
February	980.42
January	1,209.89
April	3,452.34
March	4,654.68

Calculating increases and decreases

In your assessment you could be asked to calculate a change between two numbers. For example you could be asked to calculate the increase or decrease in Jazz's bank balance each month. To calculate the change you need to subtract the previous month's balance from the month end balance for each-month as shown below (figures in brackets are a decrease):

	January	February	March	April	May	June
	£	£	£	£	£	£
Balance	1,209.89	980.42	4,654.68	3,452.34	(1,983.21)	(867.32)
Change	Note	(229.47)	3,674.26	(1,202.34)	(5,435.55)	1,115.89

Note We cannot calculate the change for January as we have not been provided with a figure for the previous month.

You need to be particularly careful when a calculation includes a negative figure. For example the change in June is (£867.32) – (£1,983.21) = £1,115.89. You must be careful to enter the values into your calculator as negative numbers or you will not get the correct answer.

Calculating a range

Another task you may be asked to perform in your assessment is to calculate the range for a series of numbers. This is similar to calculating the change in two numbers that we just looked at. The range is the difference (or change) between the lowest and highest values in a series.

Range = Highest value – Lowest value

The range of Jazz's month-end balances is £4,654.68 – (£1,983.21) = £6,637.89.

You could check this is correct by adding the range to the lowest value to get the highest value.

Lowest value + Range = Highest value

(£1,983.21) + £6,637.89 = £4,654.68

Rounding numbers

It is not always necessary to provide numerical information in full detail. In your assessment you could be asked to round to the nearest whole number or to two decimal places.

For example, the number of pence in each month-end balance is unlikely to be important for any business decisions relying on this information. Therefore it may be more convenient to reduce the detail by rounding. So you could be asked to identify Jazz's highest month-end balance to the nearest £ (the nearest whole number).

When rounding to the nearest whole number you must apply the following rule:

If the digit to the immediate right of the decimal point is 4, 3, 2 or 1, simply drop all digits that come after the decimal point.

If the digit to the immediate right of the decimal point is 5, 6, 7, 8 or 9, add one to the digit immediately before the decimal point, and drop all digits to the right of it.

So if we apply this to the highest balance of £4,654.68 the digit to the right the decimal point is 6. So we add 1 to the digit before the decimal point and drop all numbers after the decimal point. So the highest value rounded to the nearest £ (whole number) is £4,655.

Alternatively you could be asked to round a value with more decimal places to two decimal places, (equivalent to the nearest penny). For example you could be asked to calculate half of the lowest monthly balance to two decimal places.

Half of the lowest balance is (£1,983.21) ÷ 2 = (£991.605).

To round this to two decimal places is a similar process to rounding to the nearest whole number, except that you start with the second number after the decimal point which is known as the second decimal place. So the rule for rounding to two decimal places is as follows:

If the digit to the immediate right of the second decimal place is 4, 3, 2 or 1, simply drop all digits that come after the second decimal place.

If the digit to the immediate right of the second decimal place is 5, 6, 7, 8 or 9, add one to the second decimal place, and drop all digits to the right of it.

Applying this rule to the result we calculated for half of the lowest balance we get £991.61.

As long as you apply these rounding rules to any rounding questions in your assessment you will get the correct answer.

2 Using a calculator

Working with numbers in a business environment, it is important for you to be familiar with a calculator and how it works. Calculators can be simple or complicated, but the basic functions that you will use in this assessment will be the same.

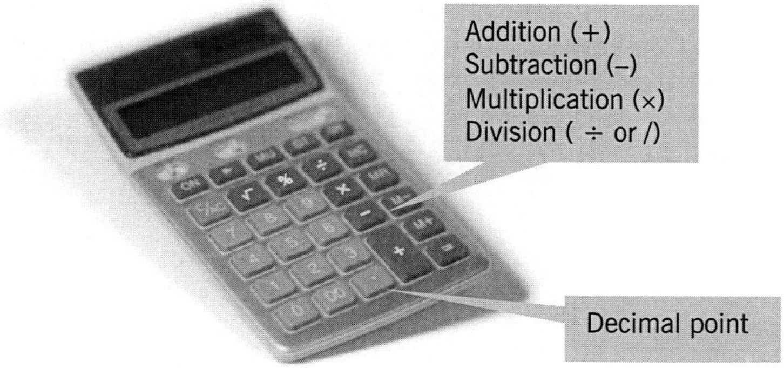

3 Addition and subtraction

In your assessment, you will be required to add numbers, both whole numbers and numbers with one or two decimal places.

Money is usually shown to two decimal places, as the numbers before the decimal point indicate the pounds and the numbers after the decimal point indicate the pence.

You may be presented with numbers in columns and have to total them.

How it works

	20,001.20
	10,020.10
	5,200.05
	2,005.02
Total	37,226.37

To add the figures together to come to the total in the shaded box, you should:

1 Enter the first figure carefully into your calculator
2 Press the + button
3 Enter the second figure
4 Press the + button
5 Enter the third figure
6 Press the + button
7 Enter the fourth figure
8 Press the = button

Ensure you enter figures carefully into your calculator, including the decimal point, or you may make an error.

Try this on the sum above and see if your answer matches ours.

In your assessment, you will be required to subtract or 'take away' numbers, both whole numbers and numbers with one or two decimal places.

How it works

You may be required to take away (subtract) one number from another; for example, as you learnt in the previous chapters, income minus cost of sales is gross profit. To determine net profit, you would then have to subtract a further number (total other expenditure).

	£
Income	100,000
Wages and salaries	20,000
Other expenditure	15,000

Profit = Income – Total expenditure

So Profit = Income – Wages and Salaries – Other expenditure:

100,000 – 20,000 – 15,000 = 65,000

To do this sum on your calculator, you should:

1 Enter the first figure, which is 100,000
2 Press the – button
3 Enter the second figure, which is 20,000
4 Press the – button
5 (The screen may currently show the gross profit figure)
6 Enter the third figure, which is 15,000
7 Press the = button (this will give the net profit figure)

In the assessment, tasks will often just ask you to 'calculate', so you must decide if addition or subtraction is required. Often a task will require both functions to be performed, such as when completing missing records (see the 'How it works' example below).

How it works

In the first example below you need to add all the figures to come to the total for parts expenditure at the bottom, which is £182,000. This is adding the column of figures, as seen above.

List of parts	£
Part A	25,000
Part B	54,000
Part C	36,000
Part D	67,000
Total (all parts)	

In the next example, you need to subtract the three given wages and salaries figures from the total figure given, to arrive at the missing administration salaries cost, which is £65 000. The easiest way is to do this in two steps, as shown in the working below the table.

List of wages/salaries costs	£
Factory 1 wages	120,000
Factory 2 wages	140,000
Administration salaries	
Directors' salaries	125,000
Total	450,000

Working:

Step one – add the three wages and salaries costs you have been given.

	£
Factory 1 wages	120,000
Factory 2 wages	140,000
Directors' salaries	125,000
Total of costs itemised	385,000

Step two – subtract this figure from the total given in the original table.

	£
Total cost	450,000
Total of costs itemised	(385,000)
Administration salaries	65,000

TASK 1 **(a)** Your organisation keeps detailed records of expenses. Motor fuel expenses for each of four delivery vehicles are shown in the table below.

Complete the table to show the total expense for motor fuel.

Delivery vehicles	Motor fuel expense
	£
Vehicle 1	128.42
Vehicle 2	196.55
Vehicle 3	86.09
Vehicle 4	112.42
Total	

(b) **Complete the table to show the expense for envelopes.** (**Note.** You may need to do this in two steps in a separate working, as shown above.)

Stationery items	Expense
	£
Ink tanks	37.50
Printer paper	18.39
Envelopes	
Pens	7.23
Total	**104.03**

(c) Last year your organisation recorded income and expenditure as shown in the table below:

Income and expenditure	£
Sales	220,000
Goods for resale	149,000
Wages	26,800
Office expenses	14,600
Selling expenses	19,100

Use the income and expenditure figures to complete the following calculations.

(i) **Calculate total expenditure.**

£

(ii) **Calculate profit.**

£

4 Multiplication and division

In your assessment you could be required to multiply or divide any two numbers, which could be a mixture of whole numbers or numbers with one or two decimal places.

If your answer comes to more than two decimal places, you will need to apply 'rounding', to two decimal places. As we saw in section 1 of this chapter rounding to two decimal places involves leaving off all the numbers after the second decimal place in your answer. All you have to remember is that, if the number in the third decimal place in your calculation is 5 or higher, you should increase the number in the second decimal place by 1.

How it works

For example, if your answer is 25.52384, you would present this as 25.52.

If your answer is 25.52684, you would present this as 25.53.

You are likely to be told that an organisation has bought a number of items at a unit price, and to work out the total price. To do this, you must multiply the price by the number of items purchased.

How it works

Your organisation purchased 5 ink cartridges at £24.95 per cartridge from Combes Stationers. **What is the total cost of the ink cartridges?**

To calculate this sum on your calculator, you should:

1 Enter the cost figure, which is 24.95
2 Press the × button
3 Enter the number of cartridges purchased, which is 5
4 Press the = button
5 The screen will now show the total cost of the ink cartridges

Alternatively, you could be told that an organisation has bought a number of items at a total price, and be asked to work out the unit price. To do this, you must divide the total price by the number of items purchased.

How it works

Your organisation purchased 30 reams of paper from Office Suppliers, for a total cost of £74.40. **What is the unit price of one ream of paper?**

To calculate this sum on your calculator, you should:

1 Enter the total cost figure, which is 74.4
2 Press the ÷ button
3 Enter the number of reams purchased, which is 30
4 Press the = button
5 The screen will now show the unit price of a ream of paper

TASK 2 Your organisation purchased 12 bottles of hand soap at £1.25 per bottle from Discount Suppliers.

(a) What is the total cost of the hand soap?

£ ______

Your organisation purchased 12 towels from Discount Suppliers, with a total cost of £52.56.

(b) What is the unit price of a towel?

£ ______

5 Calculations with time

In your assessment you may be asked to perform calculations involving common units of time. For instance, you could be asked to calculate how long a task takes or how much time is available.

Let's consider how this should be applied to the following examples.

How it works

Use the following information calculate how many man hours it takes Singh Tyres Ltd to produce each tyre:

Sing tyres produces 8,000 tyres in one week.

It employs 220 staff in the tyre production process.

Each employee works a five day week and works 8 hours per day.

Solution:

First you need to establish the total number of man hours used in the week's production:

5 × 8 × 220 = 8,800 hours.

You then need to divide this number of hours by the number of tyres produced:

8,800 ÷ 8,000 = **1.1 hours.**

How it works

The total number of working days in December in the production department is 17. Each working day is 7.5 hours. Calculate the number of free production days in December given the following jobs already scheduled.

Provide your answer to the nearest day.

Job	Items to be produced	Time per item
A	100	0.5 hours
B	20	1.3 hours

To answer this you first have to calculate the total committed production time:

100 × 0.5 + 20 × 1.3 = 76 hours.

You then need to deduct this from the total production time in December. However before you do this calculation you need to have both figures expressed in the same units. So you need the total number of hours of production time in December:

17 × 7.5 = 127.5 hours.

Now you can deduct the committed production time:

127.5 – 76 = 51.5 hours.

You were asked to provide the answer to the nearest day (remember a working day is stated as 7.5 hours:

51.5 ÷ 7.5 = 6.86 = 7 days.

What these examples show is that you may have some extra stages in calculations related to time periods connected to changing the units in which numbers are expressed. Two common reasons for this are:

- Putting your answer into the units in which you were asked to express the answer
- Expressing two time periods in the same terms before performing addition or subtraction

6 Ratios

In your assessment, you may have to calculate the ratio of one whole number to another whole number. A ratio will be presented as 'a whole number : a whole number', for example, 3 : 1. This is a way of expressing mathematically that the first number is three times bigger than the second number.

How it works

You are likely to be given a list of costs (for example, stationery items, below), and asked what the ratio of one item to the total or to another item is. You may be given a range of ratios and asked which the correct one is, as shown below.

Stationery items	Expense
	£
Ink tanks	25.00
Printer paper	13.29
Envelopes	15.11
Pens	21.60
Total	75.00

Which of the following is the ratio of the total expense for stationery items to the expense for ink tanks?

- 2:1
- 3:1
- 4:1

To calculate this, divide the total expense by the expense of ink tanks. On your calculator, you should:

1 Enter the total expense figure, which is 75
2 Press the ÷ button
3 Enter the figure for ink tanks, which is 25
4 Press the = button
5 This gives the answer 3, so the ratio is 3:1. In other words, the total expense is three times bigger than the cost of ink tanks.

TASK 3 Your organisation has the following costs relating to light and heat.

	£
Light	200,000
Heat	100,000
Total	300,000

Which of the following is the ratio of the total cost for light and heat to the cost for heat?

Options:

2:1
3:1
4:1

7 Proportions as fractions

In your assessment you might be required to calculate the proportion of one whole number to another whole number and the answer might result in a fraction. This is an expression of the relationship between the two numbers, for example, that directors' salaries equal half of total salary costs for an organisation.

How it works

You could be given the costs for the same items as above and asked what proportion of total stationery costs the ink tanks are.

Stationery items	Expense
	£
Ink tanks	20.00
Printer paper	13.29
Envelopes	25.11
Pens	21.60
Total stationery costs	80.00

As the amount for ink tanks is smaller than the total stationery costs, the answer is going to be a fraction. This fraction would be presented initially as $\frac{20}{80}$. However, fractions should always be presented in the smallest numbers possible.

To do this, you need to find a number that both numbers in the fraction can be divided by. In simple cases, the bottom number will be divisible by the top number (which means you will be able to divide the bottom number by the top number and the answer will be a whole number). You should take the following steps:

1 Take the initial fraction $\frac{20}{80}$
2 Determine whether the bottom number can be divided by the top number
3 Enter 80 into the calculator
4 Press the ÷ button
5 Enter 20 into the calculator
6 Press the = button
7 The calculator displays 4

So in this instance, the bottom number **is** divisible by the top number. This can be presented as follows:

$$\frac{20}{80} \div \frac{20}{20} = \frac{1}{4}$$

The answer is therefore $\frac{1}{4}$

In the exam you could be expected to calculate the following simple fractions:

- $\frac{1}{2}$
- $\frac{1}{4}$
- $\frac{1}{5}$
- $\frac{1}{10}$

TASK 4 Your organisation has the following costs for catering supplies.

	£
Tea	75
Coffee	250
Milk	425
Total	750

What proportion of the total cost is made up by tea?

8 Percentages

In your assessment, you may be required to calculate what percentage one figure is of another. The answer may be a whole number, or a number to one or two decimal places.

A simple example of a percentage is that '75% of the population drinks tea'. What this means is that out of every 100 people in the population, 75 of them drink tea. Accordingly, 25 of them don't, so you could also say that 25% of the population does not drink tea.

Calculating a percentage in this way can give more user-friendly information than if you were told that the population is 61,792,000, of which 46,344,000 drink tea.

In the same way, it might be more useful for directors of an organisation to be told that, for every £100 earned, £25 is profit (25%) – rather than just being told that for total income of £37,794,584, profit is £9,448,646.

How it works

You might be given figures for sales and expense, for example:

	£
Sales	120,000
Expenses	90,000
Profit	30,000

You may then be asked to calculate profit as a percentage of sales. To calculate this on your calculator, you should:

1 Enter the profit figure, which is 30,000

2 Press the ÷ button

3 Enter the sales figure, which is 120,000

4 Press the = button

5 The screen should show a figure after the decimal place, 0.25

6 Press the × button

7 Enter 100

8 Press the = button

9 The screen will show the percentage figure (in this case, 25%). In other words, for every £100 earned, the organisation makes £25 profit.

Alternatively, you may be given a figure (for example, a sales price) and be told that it is going to increase by a certain percentage. You may be asked what the amount of the increase is.

How it works

You might be told that the sales price for Part AB23 is £4.80 and that it is going to increase by 5%. You could be required to calculate the amount of the rise.

The best way to understand this is to say that £4.80 is 100%. You can calculate what 1% is by dividing the price by 100. You can then find 5% by multiplying by 5. To calculate the figure, you therefore need to:

1 Enter the existing price, which is 4.80
2 Press the ÷ button
3 Enter 100
4 Press the = button
5 The screen shows 1%, which is 0.048
6 Press the × button
7 Enter 5
8 Press the = button
9 The screen shows 5%, which is 0.24

The increase is 24 pence (you would show this in the assessment as £0.24).

TASK 5 **(a)** Your organisation has produced the following figures for the year.

	£
Sales	253,700
Expenses	190,275
Profit	63,425

Calculate profit as a percentage of sales.

[ ] %

(b) The current selling price of part DC45IT is £569. This is going to increase by 3%.

Calculate the increase in the selling price to the nearest penny.

£ [ ]

9 Fractions

Similarly in your assessment, you might be asked to apply a fraction to a whole number. This may give an answer which is a whole number, or a number to one or two decimal places.

How it works

You might be told the current selling price of an item and be told that it is going to rise by a fraction. For example, the current selling price of part AX345 is £36. It is going to rise by $\frac{1}{6}$. What is the increase in selling price for part AX345?

To calculate this figure on your calculator, you need to:

1 Enter the existing price, which is 36
2 Press the × button
3 Enter the top number in the fraction, which is 1
4 Press the ÷ button
5 Enter the bottom number in the fraction, which is 6
6 Press the = button
7 The screen shows the increase in the selling price, which is 6

Steps 2 and 3 are NOT absolutely necessary when the top number of the fraction is 1, but are necessary if the top number is higher than 1 for example where the fraction is 2/3.

TASK 6 **(a)** The current selling price of part XZ20 is £49. This is going to increase by $\frac{1}{4}$.

Calculate the increase in the selling price.

£

(b) The current selling price of part CVB34 is £25. This is going to increase by $\frac{1}{5}$.

Calculate the increase in the selling price.

£

10 Converting percentages, fractions and decimals

The relationship between two values can be expressed as either a fraction, a decimal or a percentage. Your assessment questions may require you to convert a value expressed one way into another form – for instance converting a fraction such as ½ into a percentage (50%) or a decimal (0.5).

Percentages, fractions and decimals are different ways of expressing the same thing. One per cent is $\frac{1}{100}$ as a fraction and 0.01 as a decimal. We can use this fact to convert between the different ways to express a value.

Fractions and percentages

If you are asked to convert a percentage into a fraction, for example 25%, first convert this to a number of hundredths: $\frac{25}{100}$. Then divide the top number into the bottom one, $100 \div 25 = 4$. This is the bottom of the fraction and the top will be 1, giving $\frac{1}{4}$.

To convert a fraction into a percentage divide the bottom of the fraction into 100. So, to convert $\frac{1}{5}$ into a percentage, $100 \div 5 = 20\%$.

Percentage and decimals

In a decimal value the first two decimal places equates to a number of hundredths. So 0.25 could be described as twenty-five hundredths. We already know that percentages are just hundredths, so 0.25 is equal to 25%. You just need to multiply the decimal by 100. So $0.25 \times 100 = 25\%$.

It is equally easy to convert in the opposite direction. You simply need to divide the percentage to get a decimal. So 250% is $250 \div 100 = 2.5$.

Decimals and fractions

To convert a decimal to a fraction first multiply by 100 then divide the result into 100. If this gives a whole number then this is the bottom of the fraction with 1 on the top. For example if you need to convert 0.2 into a fraction, multiply by 100: $0.2 \times 100 = 20$.

Divide this result into 100, $100 \div 20 = 5$.

So the fraction is $\frac{1}{5}$.

To convert a fraction into a decimal divide the bottom of the fraction into 100, then divide by 100. Using $\frac{1}{5}$,

$100 \div 5 = 20$

$20 \div 100 = 0.2$.

In order to get comfortable with converting between these ways of presenting numerical information you need to practice as many examples as possible.

TASK 7 A company has the following types of expenditure.

Expense	£
Selling	2,300
Distribution	11,500
Administration	9,200

Calculate the proportion of total expenditure made up of selling expenses. Express your answer as a:

Fraction

Decimal

Percentage

11 Averages

In your assessment, you may have to calculate the average value. An average gives an indication of typical values in a series of numbers. There are two averages which you need to be able to calculate. They are the mean and the mode.

Mean

The mean that you calculate may be a whole number or a decimal which you could also be asked to round. The mean cost of five units, for instance, is the total cost divided by the number of elements making up that cost (5); that is what the individual unit cost would be if they were all the same. It is critical therefore to work out how many elements make up the total, in order to do the calculation.

How it works

You may be given a range of costs, with a total, and asked what the mean average cost is. For example, the following are the costs of wages per department in your organisation. There are four elements (departments) making up the total cost.

	£
Department 1	253,049
Department 2	645,900
Department 3	234,984
Department 4	302,845
Total	1,436,778

To calculate the average cost per department on your calculator, you need to:

1 Enter the total cost, which is £1,436,778
2 Press the ÷ button
3 Enter the total number of departments being averaged (in this case 4)
4 Press the = button
5 The screen should show the average cost per department, which is £359,194.50

The key thing to remember when calculating the mean is that the number you divide by is the number of things being averaged. This will never be more than 5 in your assessment, but could be 2, 3 or 4.

If you had been asked for the average to the nearest whole number you would need to apply rounding.

The number to the right of the decimal point is 5. Following the rule for rounding covered earlier in this chapter you must add 1 number before the decimal point, and drop the digits after the decimal point.

This gives an answer of £359,195.

TASK 8 The following table shows the number of miles driven by the three delivery vehicles belonging to your organisation during the year:

Delivery vehicles	Mileage
	£
Vehicle 1	2,645
Vehicle 2	1,035
Vehicle 3	895
Total	4,575

Calculate the average number of miles driven by the delivery vehicles.

[ ] miles

Mode

The mode is different type of average. The mode is the most frequently occurring value. As an example assume the following series of values is the number of out-of-stock customer orders in a week:

Week 1	7
Week 2	0
Week 3	3
Week 4	3
Week 5	4
Week 6	8
Week 7	4
Week 8	1
Week 9	3
Week 10	11

Looking at this information you can see that there are three weeks when the number of stockouts is 3. This is the most commonly occurring value and so it is the mode.

The mode is not necessarily just one value. If the number of stockouts in week 10 had been 4 rather than 11 the mode would be 3 and 4. This is an important difference to the mean which is always a single value, although not necessarily one that was actually recorded. The mean number of stockout is 4.4, but you can see that there was not a week when 4.4 stockouts were experienced.

Using averages to estimate a value

One use of averages is to estimate another value. For instance if you know the mean value of sales for one month you could estimate the value of sales for the year by multiplying the monthly sales by 12.

The mode can also be used to predict a value. For instance, if the mode for the number of hours of overtime worked by an employee per day over the last 30 days is 1.5 hours, this can be seen as the most likely value for the next day.

How it works

The following is the number of invoices sent out by the finance department per day for the last 5 business days together with the number of invoice queries received from customers:

	Monday	Tuesday	Wednesday	Thursday	Friday
Number of invoices	120	142	111	98	145
Number of queries	4	5	2	4	4

Estimate the number of invoices that the finance department will produce in the next 20 business days?

The daily mean can be used to estimate the number of invoices over a number of days.

Daily mean = (120 + 142 + 111 + 98 + 145) ÷ 5 = 123.2.

Estimate for 20 days 123.2 × 20 = **2,464**.

Estimate the most likely number of queries that the finance department will receive on the next business day.

The mode is the most likely value to occur = 4.

Chapter overview

Working with numbers in the business environment may involve recording values in words or figures.

Your assessment may require you to rank a series of numbers in ascending or descending order, as well as calculating increases and decreases.

You may be required to apply rounding to your answers to assessment question either to two decimal places or to the nearest whole number.

You need to be confident in the use of a calculator to perform basic mathematical functions on data provided in questions. Ensure that you enter figures carefully into your calculator, including the decimal point, or you may make an error.

Money is usually shown to two decimal places, as the numbers before the decimal point indicate the pounds and the numbers after the decimal point indicate the pence.

If you are working with units of time make sure that you provide your answer in the correct units and always perform subtraction and addition with numbers expressed in the same units.

In your assessment, you may have to express one value in terms of another. This can be done using ratios, decimals, fractions or percentages.

You may also be required to convert between these different ways of expressing the relationship between two values – for instance converting a fraction such as ½ into a percentage (50%) or a decimal (0.5).

There are two averages you may be required to calculate: the mean, which is the total of all values divided by the number of values, and the mode, which is the most frequently occurring value in a series of numbers.

In your assessment, you may need to use an average to predict or estimate a future value.

4 Using numbers in business: Test your learning

This chapter gives you question practice on the topics you covered in the previous chapter. The questions are in the same style you can expect in your assessment. You can find the answers at the back of this Workbook.

1 Your organisation sold 2 cars for £958.30 in total to Super Car Traders.

(a) **What is the average price of each car?**

£ [ ]

A third car is sold for £1200.

(b) **What percentage of total sales does the sale of the third car represent to the nearest percentage point?**

[ ] **%**

2 Last year your organisation recorded income and expenditure as shown in the table below.

Income and expenditure	£
Cash sales	380,000
Credit sales	197,500
Wages and salaries	285,900
Other expenses	197,583

(a) Use the income and expenditure figures to complete the following calculations.

(i) **Calculate total expenses:**

£ [ ]

(ii) **Calculate profit:**

£ [ ]

(b) **Using your answer from (a)(ii), calculate profit as a percentage of sales. If your answer is not a whole number, provide your answer to two decimal places.**

[ ] %

3 An organisation is reviewing the selling price of some of its products.

The current selling price of product number 52 is £17.00. This is to be increased by $\frac{1}{5}$ (one fifth).

(a) **Calculate the increase in selling price for product number 52:**

£ [ ]

The current selling price of product number 12 is £18.00. This is to be increased by 6%.

(b) **Calculate the increase in selling price for product number 12:**

£ [ ]

4 An organisation is reviewing the selling price of some of its products.

The current selling price of product number 104 is £62. This is to be increased by $\frac{1}{10}$.

(a) **Calculate the increase in selling price for product number 104:**

£ [ ]

The current selling price of product number AZ25 is £9. This is to be increased by 7.5%. Provide your answer to the nearest penny.

(b) **Calculate the increase in selling price for product number AZ25:**

£ [ ]

5 Your organisation keeps detailed records of sales.

Sales at each of four outlets are shown in the table below.

(a) **Complete the table to show the sales at Outlet 4:**

Sales per outlet	**£**
Outlet 1	250,368.25
Outlet 2	199,473.79
Outlet 3	302,699.39
Outlet 4	
Total	1,127,751.60

(b) **Calculate the average sales per outlet:**

£

Analysed sales at Outlet 1 are shown in the table below.

(c) **Complete the table to show the sales from menswear:**

Item	**£**
Menswear	
Ladieswear	61,506
Childrenswear	62,595
Household fabrics	50,076
Total	250,380

(d) **Which of the following is the ratio of total sales at Outlet 1 to sales of childrenswear at Outlet 1?**

- 4:1
- 5:1
- 6:1

(e) **Which of the following is the percentage of the total sales at Outlet 1 made up by household fabrics?**

- 20%
- 16.67%
- 14.29%

6 Your organisation keeps detailed records of costs.

Costs at each of two premises are shown in the table below.

(a) **Complete the table to show the costs at Premises 2:**

Costs per premises	**£**
Premises 1	50,924.72
Premises 2	
Total	102,049.94

(b) **Calculate the average cost for each premises:**

£

Analysed costs at Premises 1 are shown in the table below.

Item	£
Cost of sales	34,368
Distribution costs	6,372
Administration costs	10,185
Total	50,925

(c) **Which of the following is the ratio of total costs to administration costs?**

- 4:1
- 5:1
- 6:1

(d) **Express your answer to (c) as a percentage:**

%

5 Sales and purchases in business

Chapter coverage

This chapter focuses on organisations that are run to make a profit. It covers the nature of income and expenditure and how their relationship leads to a business making profits or losses. The chapter also covers the typical business processes related to sales and purchases and the documents associated with them.

1 The purpose of businesses

Not all organisations aim to make a profit, for example charities and some public sector organisations. Those that do are often referred to as businesses. As we have seen, businesses include sole traders, partnerships and companies.

Businesses exist to do something; usually this involves providing goods or services.

Income and expenditure

Businesses receive money from selling goods and services. This is known as income.

Businesses also spend money on goods and services to resell to customers and the costs of running the organisation such as employee wages or electricity. These are known as expenses.

The relationship between how much an organisation spends and how much it sells at a given price level determines whether it is successful and whether it is able to continue in business.

Profit and loss

If income exceeds expenses the organisation makes a profit. Alternatively, if expenses exceed income it will make a loss.

If a business is making a profit then it will be generating an overall inflow of money, whereas if it is loss making it will experience an overall outflow of money.

KEYWORDS

Profit is what an organisation makes if income is greater than expenditure in a financial period.

A **loss** is what an organisation makes if income is less than expenditure in a financial period.

How it works

Organisation A	
	£
Income	100,000
Expenditure	80,000
Profit	20,000

Organisation B	
	£
Income	50,000
Expenditure	75,000
Loss	(25,000)

In these examples:

Organisation A has **spent** £20,000 **less than** it **earned** in the financial period. This is therefore a **profit** for that period.

Organisation B has **spent** £25,000 **more than** it **earned** in the financial period. This is therefore a **loss** for that period.

Note that expenditure is sometimes shown in brackets to show that it is being subtracted from income.

A loss is often shown in brackets to show that it is a negative number, rather than being shown as –£25,000.

Consequences of making losses

If expenditure exceeds sales a business will make a loss. This leads to an outflow of money from the business and this will not be able to be sustained indefinitely.

Businesses need a supply of money in order to operate or they may experience the following problems:

- An inability to pay for purchases and meet other expenses such as wages.
- The business's bank account will be reduced and may go into overdraft.
- If suppliers are not paid on time, they may withdraw credit from the business.
- In the long run the business will find it difficult to carry on operating and could fail.

Opportunities from making a profit

If a business's sales exceed expenditure it will make a profit and will receive an overall inflow of money. This inflow of money can be used in a number of ways to benefit the business or its owners including:

- Further investment in the business to create growth
- Investment in the bank to earn interest
- Distribution to the business's owners

KEYWORDS

Expenses are the money a business pays out when it spends money to purchase goods or services for the organisation or to resell or to run the organisation.

Income is the money a business receives when it makes sales of goods or services to other parties.

You need to learn these definitions. Knowing what these terms mean is crucial in your assessment.

How it works

The following are examples of expenses and income.

Item	Classification	Further definition
Sales of goods	Income	Earnings resulting from selling items to customers
Providing services	Income	Customers pay for receiving a service
Bank interest received	Income	Earnings resulting from having money saved in the bank
Purchases (raw materials or goods for resale)	Expenses	Expenditure on items to produce or sell to customers
Payments to staff	Expenses	Wages and salaries paid to staff working in the business
Insurance	Expenses	Payments to insure assets against loss or damage

Item	Classification	Further definition
Advertising	Expenses	Payments made to advertise an organisation's products
Road tax/fuel/motor expenses	Expenses	Payments made to use the organisation's vehicles

Note about expenditure: there could be a large number of examples of different services an organisation spends money on. Only a small number have been given here to illustrate – try to think of some more in an organisation with which you are familiar.

TASK 1 Place the items listed below into the appropriate box.

advertising cost, sale, insurance, fuel costs, interest received, interest on a bank overdraft, wages and salaries

Expenses
Income

2 Sales and purchases

Nearly all businesses seeking to make a profit will make sales and purchases. You need to learn the terminology related to sales and purchases, know typical payments terms and understand their effect on a business's bank account.

Sales

Businesses sell goods to other businesses and individuals. These parties are generally referred to as customers.

A client is someone who engages a professional to provide a service. Therefore someone who uses the services of a lawyer, accountant or a plumber would typically be referred to as a client rather than as a customer.

However, it should be noted that in practice the terms client and customer can be applied rather loosely and are often used interchangeably.

Cash and credit sales

A customer of a retail shop generally pays for the goods purchased immediately. This is an example of a cash sale.

Alternatively, an organisation may not receive payment for goods or services it sells straightaway because it has extended **credit** to the customer or client. For example many mobile phone subscriber pay their account in monthly after the service has been provided. This is because the mobile phone operator has extended credit to them.

Where credit sales are made, the terms of the sale will specify the period of time within which the customer or client has to make payment. We will consider this more when we look at payment terms below.

KEYWORDS

A **customer** is a person or business who buys goods or services.

A **client** is a person who engages the services of a professional.

A **cash sale** is a transaction to sell goods or services for which payment is made immediately.

A **credit sale** is a transaction to sell goods or services when payment is made at a later date than the delivery of goods or provision of the service.

Purchases

A business will also purchase good and services. The individual from whom a business buys goods and services is known as a supplier. For example, nearly all businesses will use electricity and therefore will have an electricity company as one of their suppliers.

Just as we saw with sales, purchases may be made on a cash basis requiring immediate payment or on a credit basis where payment is made at a later date than the delivery of goods or services.

If a business needs to purchase goods or a service there will often be a large number of potential suppliers. In order to simplify the purchasing process a business may have a list of approved suppliers. These will be suppliers where the business has verified their ability to supply appropriate goods or services at an acceptable price. For example, if a business has a water leak and needs the services of a plumber, rather than having to set about finding a plumber and establishing whether they are reliable and can provide good service at a reasonable price it will be much more efficient to call a plumber from a list of approved suppliers.

KEYWORDS

A **supplier** is a person who sells goods and services to a customer.

A **cash purchase** is a transaction to purchase goods or services for which payment is made immediately.

A **credit purchase** is a transaction to purchase goods or services when payment is made at a later date than the delivery of goods or provision of the service.

Payment terms

Where goods and services are purchased and sold, the payment terms for the transaction will be agreed by the business and the other party.

The purpose of establishing payment terms for a transaction is to ensure that the customer or client knows when to pay invoices by and to ensure that suppliers are paid at an agreed time.

There are many different payment terms that might be encountered in practice. You should be aware of the following ones:

Payment terms	Meaning
In advance	Payment is required before goods are delivered or services supplied.
On delivery	Sometimes referred to as cash on delivery (or just COD). Generally used in relation to supply of goods where the customer makes payment only when the goods are delivered
Specified period after invoice date	For credit sales the terms of the transaction may specify how long the customer has to make payment after the date of the invoice. Commonly used periods include 10, 14, 30 or 60 days after the invoice date.
Payment by end of month of invoice	All invoices dated in a particular month must be paid by that month end. For example if two invoices are received, one dated 2 May and the other 24 May, both require payment by 31 May. In this situation the period of credit extended to the customer varies depending on the date of the invoice.

How it works

Paper Products is an organisation which makes printed boxes and other items. It has a customer, Applebys, and a supplier, Pearmans. It has **credit** transactions with both of them.

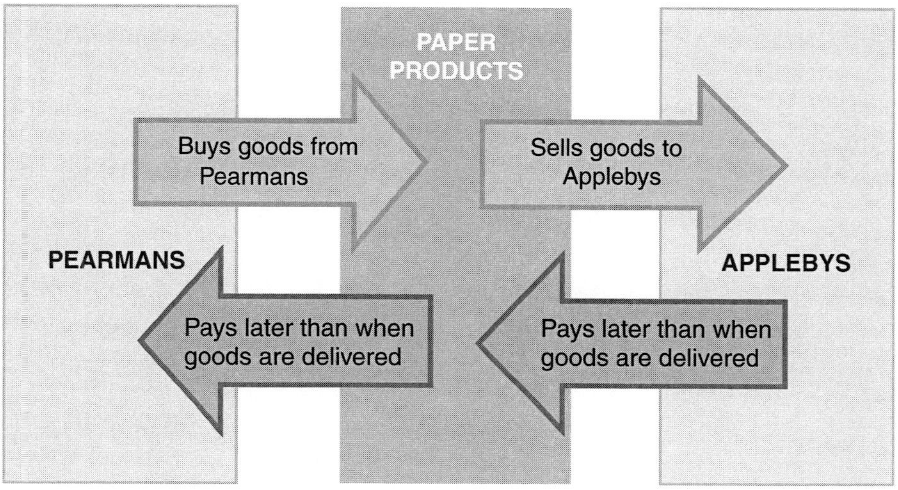

Wood Works is an organisation which makes wooden items. It has a customer, Cherryton, and a supplier, Banarama. It has **cash** transactions with both of them.

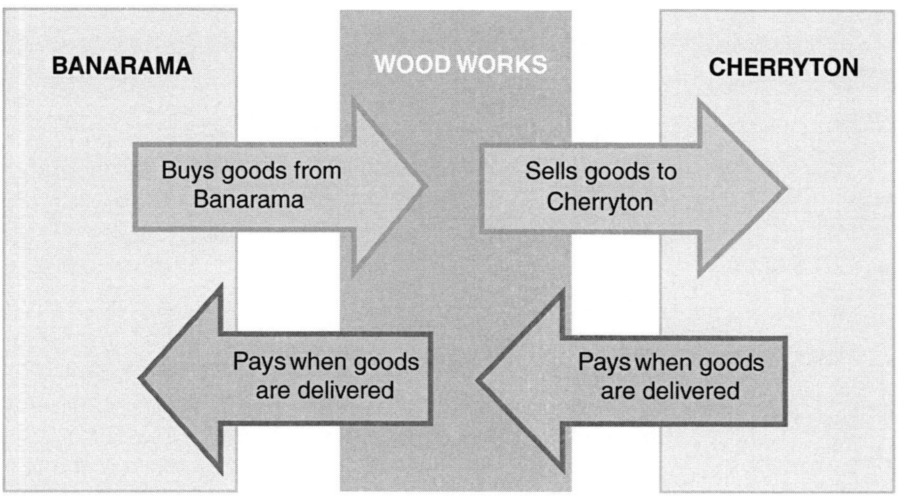

Effect of payment terms on the bank balance

Payment terms affect when a business receives payment for sales and makes payment for purchases. Because of this the payment terms of a business's transactions has an effect on its bank balance of the business.

For example, if on the same day a business makes a purchase of goods for £100 and sells them on to a customer for £120 the business has made a profit of £20. You might expect that this would lead to the business's bank balance increasing by the £20 of profit. This would be the case if both sale and purchase were for cash. However, assume that the payment terms for the purchase were cash on delivery and for the sale 30 days after invoice date. In this situation the business pays out £100 immediately and may only receive the £120 from the sale 30 days after the invoice date. Therefore the business's bank balance would fall by £100 until payment is received for the sale, which could take 30 days.

TASK 2 Place the items listed below into the appropriate box.

Sale of goods when payment is made at a date later than delivery
Sale of goods when cash is paid on delivery
Sale of services when cash is paid at a date later than the service was provided
Sale of services when cash is paid on delivery of the service
Purchase of goods when payment is made at the same time as delivery of the goods
Purchase of services when payment is made at the same time as the service is provided
Purchase of goods when payment is made at a date later than delivery
Purchase of a service when payment is made at a later date than the service is provided

Cash sale	**Credit sale**
Cash purchase	**Credit purchase**

TASK 3 (a) The balance of an organisation's income and expenditure results in profit or loss.

Which ONE of the following statements is true?

When income exceeds profit, an organisation has made a loss.	☐
When income exceeds expenditure, an organisation has made a profit.	☐
When income exceeds expenditure, an organisation has made a loss.	☐

(b) The balance of an organisation's income and expenditure results in profit or loss.

Which ONE of the following statements is true?

When expenditure exceeds profit, an organisation has made a loss. ☐

When expenditure exceeds income, an organisation has made a profit. ☐

When expenditure exceeds income, an organisation has made a loss. ☐

(c) Which one of the following would increase a business's bank balance?

Reducing the period of time before customers have to pay ☐

Agreeing to pay suppliers in cash, rather than on credit ☐

Increasing the proportion of credit sales ☐

(d) Which one of the following would NOT be a likely consequence of a business making losses?

Insufficient money to make purchases ☐

The ability to increase investment in the business ☐

An overdraft on the business's bank account ☐

(e) Using the information in the first two tables, place a tick in the appropriate column of the third table below to show whether each of the organisations has made a profit or a loss. You should not place more than one tick (✓) against each organisation.

Organisation A	
	£
Income	80,000
Expenditure	70,000

Organisation B	
	£
Income	150,000
Expenditure	120,000

Organisation	Profit	Loss
Organisation A		
Organisation B		

3 Business procedures and documents

Organisations have standardised procedures related to both sales and purchases. These procedures aim to standardise the way in which purchases and sale are done, regardless of the staff members involved.

As part of its business procedures for sales and purchases a business will use a number of different types of documents.

The objectives of standardised business procedures are:

- **The prevention of errors**: Procedures help to ensure that all relevant information is provided and can incorporate authorisation checks.
- **The promotion of efficiency**: Using consistent procedures and filling out standard documentation is easier than starting from scratch. Greater efficiency reduces the likelihood of missing deadlines.
- **To ensure that all necessary information is collected**: A business will require certain information for accounting and tax purposes. Documentation can be designed to ensure that this information is captured.
- **To avoid disputes with customers and suppliers:** Preparing standard documents containing all the relevant information related to a transaction reduces the chance of a disagreement with a customer or supplier and helps to promote good customer/supplier relations.

Any system is only effective if it is adhered to. Therefore it is important that all members of an organisation's staff follow procedures carefully. This incudes filling out any documents accurately and in full. It may be tempting to 'cut corners' and not complete documents properly. This might involve:

- Not completing documents in full
- Not obtaining required authorisations
- Not completing documents on time

However, you should avoid such practices as this can lead to problems such as errors, disputes and incorrect information and in the long run reduce business efficiency.

Business procedures for sales

For credit sales the process starts with an order from a customer. The **customer order** could be received from the customer by mail or email or the order could be received by phone and recorded on a standardised form. This form will record the details of the goods or services that the customer wishes to buy.

If the transaction relates to the supply of goods, when the goods are sent to the customer they will be accompanied by a **delivery note** which contains details of what has been supplied and describes the order to which they relate.

A **sales invoice** will then be generated describing the goods supplied, the order it relates to and the amount due and specifying the payment terms. When payment is received from the customer the business will record this income.

We will look at exactly what information these documents should contain in a moment.

Documents used in credit sales

Customer		Business
	→	Customer order
	←	Delivery note
	←	Sales invoice

Business procedures for purchases

Firstly, a supplier must be selected. Most organisations will maintain an approved supplier list from which a supplier must be selected. If there is not an approved supplier for the goods or services required there is typically an authorisation process to ensure the supplier is appropriate.

Next the organisation raises a **purchase order** which it sends to the selected supplier.

The organisation will then receive the goods or services requested. The organisation will receive a **delivery note** from the supplier along with the goods. The supplier typically requires someone at the business to sign a copy of the delivery note to acknowledge that the goods were received in good condition.

Goods are likely to be received into a warehouse or goods inwards department. This department will check and record what has been delivered, compare it to the delivery note and record any discrepancy. An internal document recording goods received will be raised (known as a **goods received note**, GRN) and is evidence that the goods ordered were received. A comparison of a GRN to the purchase order will reveal any discrepancies in what was delivered compared to what was ordered. Any such discrepancies will need to be queried with the supplier.

After the goods have been delivered the supplier will send the **purchase invoice**. A business will check the GRN/delivery note against the purchase invoice and the purchase order before making payment. Otherwise there is a risk that payment will be made for goods that haven't been received or were not ordered in the first place.

Having satisfied itself that the invoice related to goods both ordered and delivered payment will be made and the expenditure will be recorded.

Documents used in credit purchases

Supplier (approved supplier list)		Business
	←	Purchase order
	→	Delivery note
	→	Purchase invoice

TASK 4 **Identify which one of the statements below is correct.**

A goods received note is produced by a supplier. ☐

A delivery note should state the purchase order number. ☐

A purchase invoice should state the customer order number. ☐

An customer invoice should always require payment before goods are delivered. ☐

KEYWORDS

A **purchase invoice** is the document a supplier gives an organisation in relation to a purchase of goods on credit. It indicates the amount owed and when that amount is due for payment.

A **sales invoice** is the document a business gives a customer in relation to a sale of goods on credit. It indicates the amount owed and when that amount is due for payment.

A **purchase order** is the document a business provides to a supplier requesting that the supplier sells the organisation the goods stated on the order.

A **customer order** is the document a business receives from a customer requesting that the organisation sells the goods stated on the order.

A **delivery note** is the document accompanying goods when they are delivered. It describes the goods being delivered and the order and invoice they relate to.

A **goods received note (GRN)** when the goods ordered by a business are received the GRN is prepared recording the details of what was received. This is an internal document and should be compared to the invoice before payment.

Note. An organisation is both a customer and a supplier – so, for example, it will both receive and send both orders and invoices.

How it works

Here are examples of the documents described above:

INVOICE	**Invoice number 56314**		
Haywood Distributors **Industrial Estate** **Haywood HY4 2SK** **Tel: 01234 563939**			
VAT registration:	0274 2694 49		
Date/tax point:	7 September 20XX		
Order number:	32011		
Customer:	Freeway Superstores 28 Liberty Park Haywood HY4 5TR		
Account number (customer code)	HD 35		
Description/product code	**Quantity**	**Unit amount** **£**	**Total** **£**
Sondy Flat Screen TVs /3200IST25	6	300.00	1,800.00
Net total			1,800.00
VAT at 20%			360.00
Invoice total			2,160.00
Terms 30 days net			

Supplier

Invoice date

Customer

Items being sold

Tax

Period after which payment is due

ORDER

Customer

FREEWAY SUPERSTORES
28 Liberty Park
Haywood HY4 5TR
Tel 0303446 Fax 0303447

To: Haywood Distributors
Industrial Estate
Haywood
HY4 2SK

Number: 32011

Date: 5 Sept 20XX

Delivery address: Freeway Superstores
28 Liberty Park
Haywood HY4 5TR

Product code	Quantity	Description	Unit list price £
4425	6	Sondy Flat Screen TVs	300 (excluding VAT)

Items to be bought

Authorised by: *P. Winterbottom* **Date:** *5 Sept 20XX*

DELIVERY NOTE **Number: HAY0345**

Deliver to:	**Supplier:**
Freeway Superstores 28 Liberty Park Haywood HY4 5TR	Haywood Distributors Industrial Estate Haywood HY4 2SK Tel: 01234 563939
Date: 6 September 20XX	
Account number (customer code)	**HD 35**

ner

Supplier

Order number	**Description**	**Unit price**	**Quantity**	**Total Price (net)**	**VAT**	**Total Price (Gross)**
32011	Sondy Flat Screen TV	300	6	1800	360	2160
Total			6	1800	360	2160

ms
red

Received in good condition.

Name:	**Signature:**

Discrepancies or damage noted

Signed by staff membe to acknowledge receip

GOODS RECEIVED NOTE

Supplier

Delivery from: Haywood Distributors Industrial Estate Haywood HY4 2SK	**GRN Number:**	**00394**	
	Supplier code:	**02-756**	
Date received:	**6 September 20XX**		
Account number (customer code)	**HD 35**		

List items received

Order number	Description	Unit price	Quantity	Total Price (net)	VAT	Total Price (Gross)
32011	Sondy Flat Screen TV	300	6	1800	360	2160
Total			6	1800	360	2160

Received by:

....

Signed by staff member

You need to know the purpose of each of the document types above, the information they contain and be able to identify errors and discrepancies.

TASK 5 The invoice below has been received from a supplier.

INVOICE	**Invoice number 2389**		
EZ Stationary Supplies **Church Lane** **Woodfield WF4 8GT** **Tel: 02143 555009**			
VAT registration:	0345 7688 21		
Date/tax point:	12 June 20XX		
Order number:	1204		
Customer:	General Builders Ltd 13E South Street Woodfield WF7 9HJ		
Account number (customer code)	GB/134		
Description/product code	**Quantity**	**Unit amount** **£**	**Total** **£**
A4 Photocopy paper – Ream	50	3.50	192.50
Net total			192.50
VAT at 20%			38.50
Invoice total			231.00
Payment terms – End of invoice month			

(a) What information is missing from this invoice?

The purchase order number	☐
The GRN number	☐
The order date	☐

(b) Once you have obtained the purchase order number which of the following is the appropriate action in respect of this invoice?

The amount of £231 should be paid by the end of June.	☐
The invoice amount should be queried with the supplier.	☐
The amount of £192.50 should be paid by the end of June.	☐

You need to know the purpose of each of the document types above, the information they contain and be able to identify errors and discrepancies.

Chapter overview

Organisations usually exist to do something. Many organisations buy and sell things.

You must learn the definitions of expenditure and income, profit and loss and understand them well enough to do simple calculations.

Businesses make both sales and purchases. You need to know terminology related to sales and purchases as well as typical payments terms and understand their effect on a business's bank account.

Organisations make both cash and credit transactions. A credit transaction is when payment is delayed over a prearranged period.

Businesses have standard business processes in relation to sales and purchases and these will involve a number of standard document types.

The key documents in relation to sales are:

- Customer order
- Delivery note
- Sales invoice

The key documents in relation to purchases are:

- Purchase order
- Delivery note
- Goods received note
- Purchase invoice

You need to know the purpose of each information they include and be able to identify errors and discrepancies.

.

Keywords

EXPENSES are the money a business pays out when it spends money to purchase goods or services for the organisation or to resell or to run the organisation.

INCOME is the money a business earns when it makes sales of goods or services to other parties.

A **LOSS** is what an organisation makes if income is less than expenditure in a financial period.

PROFIT is what an organisation makes if income is greater than expenditure in a financial period.

A **CASH PURCHASE** is a transaction to purchase goods or services when payment is made immediately.

A **CASH SALE** is a transaction to sell goods or services when payment is made immediately.

A **CLIENT** is a person who engages the services of a professional.

A **CREDIT PURCHASE** is a transaction to purchase goods or services when payment is made at a later date than the delivery of goods or provision of the service.

A **CREDIT SALE** is a transaction to sell goods or services when payment is made at a later date than the delivery of goods or provision of the service.

A **CUSTOMER** is a person who buys goods or services.

A **CUSTOMER ORDER** is the document a business receives from a customer requesting that the organisation sells the goods stated on the order.

A **DELIVERY NOTE** is the document accompanying goods when they are delivered. It describes the goods being delivered and the order and invoice they relate to.

A **GOODS RECEIVED NOTE (GRN)** When the goods ordered by a business are received, the GRN is prepared recording the details of what was received. This is an internal document and should be compared to the invoice before payment.

A **PURCHASE INVOICE** is the document a supplier gives an organisation in relation to a purchase of goods on credit. It indicates the amount owed and when that amount is due for payment.

A **PURCHASE ORDER** is the document a business provides to a supplier requesting that the supplier sells the organisation the goods stated on the order.

A **SALES INVOICE** is the document a business gives a customer in relation to a sale of goods on credit. It indicates the amount owed and when that amount is due for payment.

A **SUPPLIER** is a person who sells goods and services to a customer.

6 Sales and purchases in business: Test your learning

This chapter gives you question practice on the topics you covered in the previous chapter. The questions are in the same style you can expect in your assessment. You can find the answers at the back of this Workbook.

1 Organisations have income and expenses.

(a) **Select the appropriate word from the list of terms below to match the description.**

Description	Term described
Money spent by the organisation	
Money earned by the organisation	

List of terms

Income
Expenses

(b) **Select the appropriate word from the list of terms below to match the description.**

Description	Term described
An amount paid to purchase motor insurance	
A sale to a customer on credit	

List of terms

Expense
Income

2 Organisations can make sales and purchases for cash or for credit.

Complete the following sentences by selecting the most appropriate option from the list of terms below.

When an organisation sells goods to a customer and the customer pays for the goods three weeks after the goods are delivered, this is known as a

[ ].

When an organisation buys services from a person and pays that person on the day the service is carried out, this is known as a

[ ].

List of terms

credit sale
cash sale
credit purchase
cash purchase

3 Organisations issue and receive different documents as part of the business procedures related to buying and selling goods.

Complete the following sentences by selecting the most appropriate option from the list of terms below.

An organisation sends [ ] to a customer for goods sold on credit.

An organisation gets [ ] from a supplier accompanying goods it receives.

An organisation receives [ ] from a customer requesting that goods specified are sold to the customer.

List of terms

an invoice
a purchase order
a delivery note
a customer order
a goods received note

4 An electronics retail business sells three laptop computers to a customer on 23 August on credit and the following invoice has been prepared.

INVOICE	**Invoice number 56314**	
Select Computers Ltd **Newtown Industrial Park** **Newtown NT14 7GG** **Tel: 0786 55449867**		
VAT registration:	0274 2694 49	
Date/tax point:	7 September 20XX	
Customer:	Bilal's Office Services 2 Church Road Newtown NT3 7DH	
Account number (customer code)	HD 35	
Description/product code		**Total** **£**
Acme S34 Laptops		1,800.00
Net total		1,800.00
VAT at 20%		360.00
Invoice total		2,160.00
Payment terms 21 days		

(a) **Identify TWO items missing from the invoice prepared by Select Computers Ltd from the list below.**

Purchase order number	☐
Quantity supplied	☐
Customer order number	☐
Date goods received	☐
Date goods despatched	☐
Condition of goods received	☐

(b) **Before payment which of the following documents should Bilal's Office Services compare the invoice to?**

Customer order and goods received note	☐
Purchase order and supplier invoice	☐
Customer invoice and delivery note	☐
Purchase order and goods received note	☐

5 A business sends an invoice in respect of goods supplied to a customer on the 1 September.

(a) **Which of the following payment terms would lead to the longest period of credit being extended to the customer?**

End of the month of invoice	☐
30 days after invoice date	☐
10 business days after invoice date	☐

(b) **Which of the following actions would not be expected to increase a business's bank balance?**

Increasing the period of credit offered to customers	☐
Increasing the amount of sales	☐
Reducing the amount of purchases	☐
Increasing the amount of time taken to pay suppliers	☐

6 A business receives more goods from a supplier than it ordered.

Indicate whether the following statement is true or false.

This discrepancy should be identified by the comparing the goods received note to the purchase order.

True	☐
False	☐

7 In February 20XX General Retail Ltd has expenses of £34,509 and makes cash sales of £13,239 and credit sales of £23,446.

(a) **What is the correct figure for the profit or loss for General Retail in February?**

£ ☐

(b) All General Retail's expenses in February are paid by the end of that month. Payment terms offered by General Retail to its customers buying on credit are 60 days after invoice date.

Which of the following is true in relation to the impact of February's trading on General Retail's bank account?

It will cause it to rise.	☐
It will cause it to fall.	☐
It could cause it to fall or rise.	☐

(c) **Which ONE of the following statements is TRUE in relation to General Retail's sales?**

Deliveries of goods to credit customers are always accompanied by a sales invoice.	☐
Payments from credit customers should be checked to goods received notes.	☐
Goods should only be despatched after payment from credit customers has been received.	☐
Customers will raise a query with General Retail if the quantity of goods recorded on a GRN doesn't match the amount ordered.	☐

Chapter tasks: answers

Chapter tasks: answers

Chapter 1

Task 1

Limited companies aim to make a **profit**.

The National Health Service does not exist to make a **profit**.

Task 2

A travel agent	**Services**
A maker of musical instruments	**Manufacturing**
An online bookseller	**Retail**

Task 3

Making sure factory machinery is maintained	**Production**
Producing an employment contract for new staff	**Human resources**
Producing budgets for management	**Finance**

Task 4

(iv)

Informing the team leader that you have found the task assigned to you difficult and that you are falling behind schedule.

Task 5

The order of priority is:

B	A	C

Task 6

Notifying a customer who has failed to pay an invoice that you intend to take legal action.	**Letter**
Asking the sales department for the total of last week's sales.	**Email**
Discussing job performance with an employee.	**Face-to face**

Task 7

AmirS	
PASSWORD	
Computer	
@mirS1ngh23	✓

Task 8

I like to work in an office environment.	
I worked for three years as a purchase ledger clerk.	
I need a job with regular hours.	
I worked for three years selling mobile phone contracts.	✓
I have done a training course covering financial products.	✓
I speak three languages fluently.	✓

Chapter 3

Task 1

(a)

Delivery vehicles	**Motor fuel expense**
	£
Vehicle 1	128.42
Vehicle 2	196.55
Vehicle 3	86.09
Vehicle 4	112.42
Total	**523.48**

(b)

Stationery items	**Expense**
	£
Ink tanks	37.50
Printer paper	18.39
Envelopes	40.91
Pens	7.23
Total	**104.03**

(c) **(i)** Total expenditure = £149,000 + £26,800 + £14,600 + £19,100

£ **209,500**

(ii) Profit = £220,000 – 149,000 – £26,800 – £14,600 – £19,100

£ **10,500**

Task 2

(a) The total cost of the hand soap = 12 × £1.25

£ **15**

(b) The unit price of a towel = £52.56 ÷ 12

£ **4.38**

Task 3

The ratio of the total cost for light and heat to the cost for heat

3:1

Task 4

The proportion of the total cost made up by tea is $\frac{75}{750} \div \frac{75}{75}$

$\frac{1}{10}$

Task 5

(a) Profit as a percentage of sales = £63,425 ÷ £253,700 × 100

25	%

(b) The increase in the selling price = £569 ÷ 100 × 3

£	17.07

Task 6

(a) The increase in the selling price = £49 ÷ 4

£	12.25

(b) The increase in the selling price = £25 ÷ 5

£	5

Task 7

Fraction

(£11,500 + £9,200 + £2,300) ÷ £2,300

$\frac{1}{10}$

Decimal

100 ÷ 10 ÷ 100

0.1

Percentage

0.1 × 100

10	%

Task 8

The average number of miles driven by the delivery vehicles = 4,575 ÷ 3

1,525	**miles**

Chapter 5

Task 1

Expenses
advertising cost insurance fuel costs interest on a bank overdraft wages and salaries
Income
sale interest received

Task 2

Cash sale	Credit sale
Sale of goods when cash is paid on delivery. Sale of services when cash is paid on delivery of the service.	Sale of goods when payment is made at a date later than delivery. Sale of services when cash is paid at a date later than the service was provided.
Cash purchase	**Credit purchase**
Purchase of goods when payment is made at the same time as delivery of the goods. Purchase of services when payment is made at the same time as the service is provided.	Purchase of goods when payment is made at a date later than delivery. Purchase of a service when payment is made at a later date than the service is provided.

Task 3

(a) When income exceeds expenditure, an organisation has made a profit ☑

(b) When expenditure exceeds income, an organisation has made a loss ☑

(c) Increasing the proportion of credit sales ☑

(d) The ability to increase investment in the business ☑

(e)

Organisation	Profit	Loss
Organisation A	✓	
Organisation B	✓	

Task 4

A delivery note should state the purchase order number. ☑

Task 5

(a) The purchase order number ☑

(b) The invoice amount should be queried with the supplier. ☑

Test your learning: answers

Test your learning: answers

Chapter 2

1 (a) A sole trader is a **private sector** organisation.

(b) The police service **does not** aim to make a profit.

2 (a) Detailed expenditure analysis provided by the finance department of a partnership is used by the general public to make business decisions.

False ✓

(b) An organisation's ICT department provides a service to customers and suppliers.

True ✓

3 Information about pay increases held on the computer should be kept

in a password-protected file with access restricted to those who need the information.

A supplier of the organisation where you work asks you who the main customers of the organisation are. You reply:

'I am sorry but I cannot give you any information as it is confidential.'

4 Frequently arriving late for work is fine if it is because your train is late.

False ✓

Use of personal phones at work is acceptable provided that you leave the office to avoid disturbing colleagues.

False ✓

5 (a) Communicating by letter is **appropriate** for communications when **speed** is not of the highest importance.

(b) Teams work best when members are given clear goals by the team leader.

True ✓

Giving team members unrealistic deadlines will ensure that they work harder.

False ✓

6 (a) Tasks should be allocated to the time available based on their **urgency** and their **importance**.

(b) Diaries and calendars can be physical documents or computer software.

True ✓

A calendar is the most appropriate tool for making sure that you do not forget to complete a task when you are busy.

False ✓

7 (a) **Philip**

(b) ✓ Carefully prepare and check your CV and deliver it by hand.

Chapter 4

1 (a) The average price of each car = £958.30 ÷ 2

£ | 479.15 |

(b) 1,200 ÷ (1,200 + 958.3) × 100% = 56%

| 56 | %

2 (a) (i) Total expenses = £197,583 + £285,900

£ | 483,483 |

(ii) Profit = £380,000 + £197,500 – £483,483

£ | 94,017 |

(b) Profit as a percentage of sales = £94,017 ÷ £577,500 × 100

| 16.28 | %

3 (a) The increase in selling price for product number 52 = £17 × 1 ÷ 5

£ | 3.40 |

(b) The increase in selling price for product number 12 = £18 ÷ 100 × 6

£ | 1.08 |

4 (a) The increase in selling price for product number 104 = £62 × 1 ÷ 10

£ | 6.20 |

(b) The increase in selling price for product number AZ25 = £9 ÷ 100 × 7.5

£ | 0.68 |

5 (a) Sales at Outlet 4

Sales per outlet	**£**
Outlet 1	250,368.25
Outlet 2	199,473.79
Outlet 3	302,699.39
Outlet 4	**375,210.17**
Total	1,127,751.60

(b) Average sales per outlet = £1,127,751.60 ÷ 4

£ **281,937.90**

(c) Sales from menswear

Item	**£**
Menswear	**76,203**
Ladieswear	61,506
Childrenswear	62,595
Household fabrics	50,076
Total	250,380

(d) The ratio of total sales at Outlet 1 to sales of childrenswear at Outlet 1

4:1

(e) The percentage that household fabrics is of the total sales at Outlet 1

50,076 ÷ 250,380 × 100 = **20%**

6 (a) The costs at Premises 2

Costs per premises	**£**
Premises 1	50,924.72
Premises 2	**51,125.22**
Total	102,049.94

(b) Average cost per premises = £102,049.94 ÷ 2

£ **51,024.97**

(c) The ratio of total costs to administration costs

5:1

(d) Express your answer to (c) as a percentage

1 ÷ 5 × 100 = **20** **%**

Chapter 6

1 Organisations have assets, liabilities, income and expenditure.

(a)

Description	Term described
Money spent by the organisation	Expenses
Money earned by the organisation	Income

(b)

Description	Term described
An amount paid to purchase motor insurance	Expense
A sale to a customer on credit	Income

2 When an organisation sells goods to a customer and the customer pays for the goods three weeks after the goods are delivered, this is known as a **credit sale.**

When an organisation buys services from a person and pays that person on the day the service is carried out, this is known as a **cash purchase.**

3 An organisation sends **an invoice** to a customer for goods sold for credit.

An organisation gets **a delivery note** from a supplier accompanying goods it receives.

An organisation receives **a purchase order** from a customer requesting that the goods specified in the document be sold to the customer.

4 (a)

Quantity supplied ✓

Customer order number ✓

(b)

Purchase order and goods received note ✓

5 (a) 30 days after invoice date ✓

(b) Increasing the period of credit offered to customers ✓

6 This discrepancy should be identified by the comparing the goods received note to the purchase order.

True ✓

7 (a)

£ **2,176**

(b) It will cause it to fall. ✓

(c) Customers will raise a query with General Retail if the quantity of goods recorded on a GRN doesn't match the amount ordered. ✓

Practice assessments

AAT sample assessment

Task 1 [3 marks]

(a) Identify the sector of each organisation described below.

Description	Sector Charity ✓	 Manufacturing ✓	 Public ✓	 Retail ✓	 Service ✓
An organisation that uses money from donations to help the homeless					
An organisation that does bookkeeping for small businesses					
An organisation that makes parts for the car industry					

Some organisations will have many departments, with each department having different responsibilities.

(b) Choose from the list below the department that would be responsible for each task.

Task	Department
Writing a letter to a customer asking for payment of an amount owing	
Recruiting staff for the Production department	
Promoting the organisation's product range	

Production
Despatch
Finance
Sales and Marketing
Human Resources
ICT

Task 2

[3 marks]

Freya owns a computer repair business.

Link the boxes to show whether the statements below are true or false.

Statement		Option
If Freya's expenses are more than her income, she will make a profit.		True
If Freya's income is more than her expenses, she will make a profit.		False
If Freya has an equal amount of income and expenses, she will make a profit.		

Task 3

[6 marks]

JPK Ltd buys and sells goods on a cash basis and on a credit basis.

(a) Show whether JPK Ltd will describe the transactions below as a cash sale, credit sale, cash purchase or credit purchase.

Transaction	Description
A customer ordered goods from JPK Ltd and paid in cash on collection.	
A supplier delivered goods to JPK Ltd and asked for a cheque by the end of the month.	
JPK Ltd bought goods from a local warehouse and paid by cheque on collection.	
JPK Ltd provided goods to a customer and asked for payment in cash within 14 days.	

Cash sale
Cash purchase
Credit sale
Credit purchase

(b) Identify TWO reasons why JPK Ltd should agree payment terms with customers and suppliers.

Reason	✓
Customers will know when to pay JPK Ltd.	
JPK Ltd will know when to deliver goods to customers.	
Suppliers will know when to deliver goods to JPK Ltd.	
JPK Ltd can estimate how much money will be banked in a period.	

Task 4 [9 marks]

On 15 June, Pang Partners ordered goods from Green and Gray. The goods were delivered at the end of the month.

Green and Gray
Jackson Street
Corly
CR4 8JP

Date 30 June 20XX **Delivery note no.:** 0198

To:
Pang Partners
Lower High Street
Corly
CR4 2BP

160 items of Product XY as per your order number P3219 costing £2.25 each excluding VAT.

(a) Complete the invoice below. Insert options from the available lists and enter figures.

<table>
<tr><td colspan="2" align="center">Green and Gray
Jackson Street
Corly
CR4 8JP

VAT Registration No. 339 0318 00

Telephone: 01314 297737</td></tr>
<tr><td rowspan="3">To:

Pang Partners
Lower High
Street Corly
CR4 2BP</td><td>Date: 20XX</td></tr>
<tr><td>Delivery note no.:</td></tr>
<tr><td>Customer order no.:</td></tr>
<tr><td colspan="2" align="center">Invoice no. GG1169</td></tr>
<tr><td colspan="2">160 items of Product XY costing £ each</td></tr>
<tr><td colspan="2" align="right">Net: £</td></tr>
<tr><td colspan="2" align="right">VAT: £</td></tr>
<tr><td colspan="2" align="right">Total: £</td></tr>
</table>

Dates:	**Delivery note numbers:**	**Customer order numbers:**
15 June	0198	0198
30 June	P3219	P3219
	GG1169	GG1169

(b) Identify ONE other document that could have been used as a source of information to prepare the sales invoice above.

Documents	✓
Customer order	
Goods received note	
Approved supplier list	

(c) Who is the most appropriate person to authorise the sales invoice before it is sent to the customer?

Authorisation	✓
Finance Manager at Green and Gray	
Finance Manager at Pang Partners	
The person who delivered the goods	

Task 5 [3 marks]

You work in the accounting team of a department store. You have been asked to produce some calculations in relation to the number of customers that visit the store. You have been given the following information.

Number of customers that have visited the store in the last eight weeks							
Week 1	Week 2	Week 3	Week 4	Week 5	Week 6	Week 7	Week 8
750	840	560	920	730	1,240	900	840

(a) Arrange the numbers shown above in ascending order by dragging each number into the appropriate position in the table below.

Numbers of customers in ascending order							

(b) Calculate the range for the number of customers visiting the store during this period.

Range

(c) What is the mode for the number of customers visiting the store during this period?

Mode

Task 6 [6 marks]

You work in an accounting practice and have been asked to provide some information for a client. This is the information you have been given relating to the client's sales for four months.

Sales			
Month 1 (£)	Month 2 (£)	Month 3 (£)	Month 4 (£)
129,362	17,321	88,413	90,240

(a) Insert correct month from the available list and enter figures in the table below.

	Answer
Which month has the greatest increase in sales from the previous month?	
What is the total sales figure for all four months?	£
What is the average (mean) sales figure for the four months?	£

Months:

Month 1 Month 2
Month 3 Month 4

In the future, the client has asked for calculations to be provided four times a year.

(b) How often will the calculations be provided? Choose ONE answer.

Frequency	✓
Daily	
Monthly	
Quarterly	
Annually	

The client has a new product. They expect to sell 5,000 items in Year 1 and 7,125 items in Year 2. The selling price will be £2.72 per item.

(c) Calculate the amount of the expected sales for each year.

	£
Year 1	
Year 2	

Task 7 [9 marks]

You have been asked to calculate salary increases for three employees.

(a) For employees B, C and D, calculate their salary increase and new annual salary.

Employee	Current annual salary (£)	Percentage salary increase (%)	Amount of salary increase (£)	New annual salary (£)
A	19,200	3	576	19,776
B	18,250	2		
C	17,850	4		
D	22,900	5		

Employee E is to receive a salary increase of 1/10 of her current annual salary.

(b) What will be the percentage salary increase that employee E receives?

%

There are two employees who are paid for each hour they work. Their new hourly rates of pay are shown in the table below.

(c) Enter the hourly rate of pay rounded to two decimal places for employees F and G.

Employee	New hourly rate of pay (£)	New hourly rate of pay rounded to two decimal places (£)
F	6.6925	
G	7.3265	

Task 8 [6 marks]

(a) Identify the most appropriate software to use in each of the situations below.

Situations	Type of software to use			
	Email ✓	Presentation ✓	Word processing ✓	Spreadsheet ✓
Listing staff salaries in rows and columns				
Communicating the start time of tomorrow's sales meeting to colleagues				
Demonstrating health and safety training to a group of staff				
Writing a letter to a supplier				

(b) Show which TWO actions below would allow only authorised staff to access data stored on a computer.

Action	✓
Keep a backup copy of data	
Protect data with a password	
Install antivirus software on the computer	
Keep the computer in a locked room	

Task 9 [6 marks]

Brogan is thinking about applying for the following job advertised in the local newspaper.

Full-time Administration Assistant

We are looking to recruit a person with great attention to detail to work within our Accounts Department.

The successful applicant will support the work of three Assistant Accountants. Full training will be given so no previous experience is necessary, but the successful applicant must have ICT skills.

Details of terms of employment, including salary, will be supplied once applicants have been selected for interview.

If you are interested, complete an online application form by visiting mnbo.uk/application by the closing date of 29 November.

(a) Match FOUR statements from the list below to the job requirements above, and enter in the column below.

Statements	Appropriate to the job requirements
I am willing to learn new skills.	
I have worked in a factory building cars.	
I have qualifications in using spreadsheets and word processing software.	
I am taking driving lessons.	
I enjoy working in a team.	
I can be flexible with my working hours.	
I enjoy listening to music and dancing.	
I am careful to check my work.	

(b) Identify TWO actions Brogan should take to apply for the job.

Action	✓
Telephone and ask what the closing date is	
Ask a friend to check the completed application	
Write a letter of application, including a CV	
Complete the online application form	

Task 10 [6 marks]

You have been given the following details of amounts owed to credit suppliers.

Supplier	Payment to be received by supplier	Invoices to be paid	
		Invoice amount (£)	Invoice date
Anka Holdings	At end of the month of invoice date	420.55	3 November
		61.86	25 November
Court and Company	30 days after invoice date	320.40	10 November
		1,007.99	10 November
Pepper Partners	10 days from invoice date	72.68	10 December

(a) Complete the table below by:

- **Inserting the total amount to be paid to each supplier**
- **Selecting the date by which the supplier should receive the payment from the list provided**

Supplier	Amount to be paid (£)	Date supplier should receive payment
Anka Holdings		
Court and Company		
Pepper Partners		

Payment dates:

3 November
10 November
25 November
30 November
10 December
20 December
10 January
20 January

AAT sample assessment: answers

Task 1 [3 marks]

(a) Identify the sector of each organisation described below.

Description	Sector				
	Charity ✓	Manufacturing ✓	Public ✓	Retail ✓	Service ✓
An organisation that uses money from donations to help the homeless	✓				
An organisation that does bookkeeping for small businesses					✓
An organisation that makes parts for the car industry		✓			

Some organisations will have many departments, with each department having different responsibilities.

(b) Choose from the list below the department that would be responsible for each task.

Task	Department
Writing a letter to a customer asking for payment of an amount owing	Finance
Recruiting staff for the Production department	Human Resources
Promoting the organisation's product range	Sales and Marketing

Production
Despatch
Finance
Sales and Marketing
Human Resources
ICT

Task 2 [3 marks]

Freya owns a computer repair business.

Link the boxes to show whether the statements below are true or false.

If Freya's expenses are more than her income, she will make a profit. **False**

If Freya's income is more than her expenses, she will make a profit. **True**

If Freya has an equal amount of income and expenses, she will make a profit. **False**

True

False

Task 3 [6 marks]

JPK Ltd buys and sells goods on a cash basis and on a credit basis.

(a) **Show whether JPK Ltd will describe the transactions below as a cash sale, credit sale, cash purchase or credit purchase.**

Transaction	Description
A customer ordered goods from JPK Ltd and paid in cash on collection.	Cash sale
A supplier delivered goods to JPK Ltd and asked for a cheque by the end of the month.	Credit purchase
JPK Ltd bought goods from a local warehouse and paid by cheque on collection.	Cash purchase
JPK Ltd provided goods to a customer and asked for payment in cash within 14 days.	Credit sale

Cash sale
Cash purchase
Credit sale
Credit purchase

(b) Identify TWO reasons why JPK Ltd should agree payment terms with customers and suppliers.

Reason	✓
Customers will know when to pay JPK Ltd.	✓
JPK Ltd will know when to deliver goods to customers.	
Suppliers will know when to deliver goods to JPK Ltd.	
JPK Ltd can estimate how much money will be banked in a period.	✓

Task 4 [9 marks]

On 15 June, Pang Partners ordered goods from Green and Gray. The goods were delivered at the end of the month.

Green and Gray Jackson Street Corly CR4 8JP	
Date: 30 June 20XX	Delivery note no.: 0198
To: Pang Partners Lower High Street Corly CR4 2BP 160 items of Product XY as per your order number P3219 costing £2.25 each excluding VAT.	

(a) Complete the invoice below. Insert options from the available lists and enter figures.

<table>
<tr><td colspan="2">Green and Gray
Jackson Street
Corly
CR4 8JP

VAT Registration No. 339 0318 00

Telephone: 01314 297737</td></tr>
<tr><td rowspan="3">To:

Pang Partners
Lower High
Street Corly
CR4 2BP</td><td>Date: 30 June 20XX</td></tr>
<tr><td>Delivery note no.: 0198</td></tr>
<tr><td>Customer order no.: P3219</td></tr>
<tr><td colspan="2">Invoice no. GG1169</td></tr>
<tr><td colspan="2">160 items of Product XY costing £ 2.25 each</td></tr>
<tr><td colspan="2">Net: £ 360.00</td></tr>
<tr><td colspan="2">VAT: £ 72.00</td></tr>
<tr><td colspan="2">Total: £ 432.00</td></tr>
</table>

Dates:	Delivery note numbers:	Customer order numbers:
15 June	0198	0198
30 June	P3219	P3219
	GG1169	GG1169

(b) Identify ONE other document that could have been used as a source of information to prepare the sales invoice above.

Documents	✓
Customer order	✓
Goods received note	
Approved supplier list	

(c) Who is the most appropriate person to authorise the sales invoice before it is sent to the customer?

Authorisation	✓
Finance Manager at Green and Gray	✓
Finance Manager at Pang Partners	
The person who delivered the goods	

Task 5 [3 marks]

You work in the accounting team of a department store. You have been asked to produce some calculations in relation to the number of customers that visit the store. You have been given the following information.

Number of customers that have visited the store in the last eight weeks							
Week 1	Week 2	Week 3	Week 4	Week 5	Week 6	Week 7	Week 8
750	840	560	920	730	1,240	900	840

(a) Arrange the numbers shown above in ascending order by dragging each number into the appropriate position in the table below.

Numbers of customers in ascending order							
560	730	750	840	840	900	920	1,240

(b) Calculate the range for the number of customers visiting the store during this period.

Range
680

(c) What is the mode for the number of customers visiting the store during this period?

Mode
840

Task 6 [6 marks]

You work in an accounting practice and have been asked to provide some information for a client. This is the information you have been given relating to the client's sales for four months.

Sales			
Month 1 (£)	Month 2 (£)	Month 3 (£)	Month 4 (£)
129,362	17,321	88,413	90,240

(a) Insert correct month from the available list and enter figures in the table below.

	Answer
Which month has the greatest increase in sales from the previous month?	**Month 3**
What is the total sales figure for all four months?	**£325,336**
What is the average (mean) sales figure for the four months?	**£81,334**

Months:

Month 1 Month 2
Month 3 Month 4

In the future, the client has asked for calculations to be provided four times a year.

(b) How often will the calculations be provided? Choose ONE answer.

Frequency	✓
Daily	
Monthly	
Quarterly	✓
Annually	

The client has a new product. They expect to sell 5,000 items in Year 1 and 7,125 items in Year 2. The selling price will be £2.72 per item.

(c) Calculate the amount of the expected sales for each year.

	£
Year 1	13,600
Year 2	13,600

Task 7 [9 marks]

You have been asked to calculate salary increases for three employees.

(a) For employees B, C and D, calculate their salary increase and new annual salary.

Employee	Current annual salary (£)	Percentage salary increase (%)	Amount of salary increase (£)	New annual salary (£)
A	19,200	3	576	19,776
B	18,250	2	365	18,615
C	17,850	4	714	18,564
D	22,900	5	1,145	24,045

Employee E is to receive a salary increase of 1/10 of her current annual salary.

(b) What will be the percentage salary increase that employee E receives?

%
10

There are two employees who are paid for each hour they work. Their new hourly rates of pay are shown in the table below.

(c) Enter the hourly rate of pay rounded to two decimal places for employees F and G.

Employee	New hourly rate of pay (£)	New hourly rate of pay rounded to two decimal places (£)
F	6.6925	6.69
G	7.3265	7.33

Task 8 [6 marks]

(a) Identify the most appropriate software to use in each of the situations below.

Situations	Type of software to use			
	Email ✓	Presentation ✓	Word processing ✓	Spreadsheet ✓
Listing staff salaries in rows and columns				✓
Communicating the start time of tomorrow's sales meeting to colleagues	✓			
Demonstrating health and safety training to a group of staff		✓		
Writing a letter to a supplier			✓	

(b) Show which TWO actions below would allow only authorised staff to access data stored on a computer.

Action	✓
Keep a backup copy of data	
Protect data with a password	✓
Install antivirus software on the computer	
Keep the computer in a locked room	✓

Task 9 [6 marks]

Brogan is thinking about applying for the following job advertised in the local newspaper.

Full-time Administration Assistant

We are looking to recruit a person with great attention to detail to work within our Accounts Department.

The successful applicant will support the work of three Assistant Accountants. Full training will be given so no previous experience is necessary, but the successful applicant must have ICT skills.

Details of terms of employment, including salary, will be supplied once applicants have been selected for interview.

If you are interested, complete an online application form by visiting mnbo.uk/application by the closing date of 29 November.

(a) Match FOUR statements from the list below to the job requirements above, and enter in the column below.

Statements	Appropriate to the job requirements
I am willing to learn new skills. I have worked in a factory building cars.	I am willing to learn new skills.
I have qualifications in using spreadsheets and word processing software. I am taking driving lessons.	I have qualifications in using spreadsheets and word processing software.
I enjoy working in a team. I can be flexible with my working hours.	I enjoy working in a team.
I enjoy listening to music and dancing. I am careful to check my work.	I am careful to check my work.

(b) Identify TWO actions Brogan should take to apply for the job.

Action	✓
Telephone and ask what the closing date is	
Ask a friend to check the completed application	✓
Write a letter of application, including a CV	
Complete the online application form	✓

Task 10 [6 marks]

You have been given the following details of amounts owed to credit suppliers.

Supplier	Payment to be received by supplier	Invoices to be paid	
		Invoice amount (£)	Invoice date
Anka Holdings	At end of the month of invoice date	420.55 61.86	3 November 25 November
Court and Company	30 days after invoice date	320.40 1,007.99	10 November 10 November
Pepper Partners	10 days from invoice date	72.68	10 December

(a) Complete the table below by:

- **Inserting the total amount to be paid to each supplier**
- **Selecting the date by which the supplier should receive the payment from the list provided**

Supplier	Amount to be paid (£)	Date supplier should receive payment
Anka Holdings	482.41	30 November 1
Court and Company	1328.39	10 December 1
Pepper Partners	72.68	20 December 1

Payment dates:

3 November
10 November
25 November
30 November
10 December
20 December
10 January
20 January

BPP practice assessment 1

Task 1 [3 marks]

(a) Which ONE of the following statements is FALSE?

If sales exceed expenses a profit is made. ☐

Profit can allow a business to increase investment. ☐

Losses do not affect a business's bank account. ☐

(b) Place a tick in the appropriate column of the table below to show whether each of the items listed is an example of an income or expenditure. You should not place more than one tick (✓) against each item.

Item	Income	Expenses
Insurance		
Cash sale		
Loan interest		
Credit sale		

(c) Choose the appropriate term from the list below to match the description.

Description	Term described
A transaction to sell goods when payment is made at a later date than delivery of the goods	
A transaction to buy goods when payment is made immediately	

List of terms

Cash sale
Cash purchase
Credit sale
Credit purchase
Delivery
Expense

Task 2 **[2 marks]**

Your organisation purchased 12 boxes of paper for £60.72 in total from RG Office Supplies.

(a) What is the cost of each box of paper?

£ [ ]

RG Office Supplies agreed to issue an invoice asking your organisation to pay for the boxes of paper within 60 days.

(b) Is the purchase of the boxes of paper a cash transaction or a credit transaction?

[ ]

Task 3 **[3 marks]**

(a) Complete the following sentences by selecting the most appropriate option from the list of terms below.

An organisation receives [ ] from a supplier with goods supplied.

An organisation sends [ ] to a supplier requesting that the goods specified in the document be sold to the organisation.

List of terms

a purchase order
a goods received note
a delivery note
a purchase invoice

(b) Which of the following documents is not prepared by the seller of goods in a credit transaction?

Goods received note ☐

Customer order ☐

Sales invoice ☐

(c) **Indicate whether the following statements are true or false.**

	True	False
Customers include payment terms on customer orders stating when they are prepared to pay.	☐	☐
A service business such as a law firm usually refers to people using its services as customers.	☐	☐

Task 4 [4 marks]

(a) **Indicate the sections not properly completed in the CV below.**

Name	Jana Wozniak	
Contact details	Mobile: 0988 233 5588 65 The Pastures Laketown LK23 8ED Emial: janawoz@nmail.com	☐
Qualifications	GCSEs Maths English French Drama A levels Maths	☐
Experience	ACME Office Services I worked for ACME for 14 months from January 20X6 to March 20X7 as an accounts assistant. I left as I found it really boring and didn't pay enough.	☐
Interests	I am a keen tennis player and compete in the tennis competitions in the local area. I also enjoy computer gaming and reading.	☐

(b) **Indicate whether the following statements are true or false.**

	True	False
You would be expected to pay when using a recruitment agency to find a job.	☐	☐
The successful applicant for a job must meet all essential requirements.	☐	☐

Task 5 [3 marks]

By looking at production figures from the last year a manufacturer has calculated that on average it takes 20 minutes to produce each unit of component X and 1.25 hours to produce each unit of component Y. A customer order has been received for 75 units of component X and 15 units of component Y.

(a) Calculate the expected time to produce this order. Provide your answer in hours and minutes.

☐

(b) Which of the following would be the most effective type of deadline to motivate the production department to complete this order?

Very easily achieved ☐

Unrealistic ☐

Challenging but achievable ☐

(c) In order to complete the order the production manager decides he needs additional temporary staff.

Which is the most appropriate department to organise this?

Finance ☐

Human resources ☐

Sales and marketing ☐

IT ☐

Task 6 [3 marks]

Jamal, a new employee at David's Sock Suppliers Ltd has to choose a password to enable access to the company's computer systems.

(a) The primary reason for this is best described by which of the following?

Information and data security ☐

Confidentiality ☐

Work scheduling ☐

(b) Which of the following would be the most effective password for Jamal to select?

Computer ☐

12345 ☐

J@ma1 ☐

(c) David's Sock Supplies Ltd wishes to increase its data and information security in order to enable the company to recover its data if it were damaged or destroyed.

Which of the following would be the most appropriate action to achieve this objective?

Install anti-virus software on the IT system	☐
Introduce back-up procedures	☐
Put in place restrictions on physical access	☐

Task 7 [3 marks]

You have been asked to pay the daily takings from cash sales into Tricky Traders' bank account:

Four	£50 notes
Two	£20 notes
Four	£5 note
Twenty	50 pence coins
Fifteen	20 pence coins

(a) **What is the total amount that will be paid into the bank account?**

£ ☐

(b) **What percentage of the total amount is made up of £5 notes? Round your answer to 2 decimal places.**

☐ %

(c) **What is the ratio of the value of notes to the value of coins?**

☐

Task 8 [4 marks]

On 24 April 20XX you are preparing an invoice for three hundred and twenty-three pounds and fifty-five pence to send to a customer, Woodcutter Ltd.

(a) **Which ONE of the following options shows the date as it should be written on the invoice?**

24 April 20XY	☐
24.05.XX	☐
24 April 20XX	☐

(b) Which ONE of the following options shows the payee as it should be written on the cheque?

Woodcutters ☐

Woodcutter Ltd ☐

Woodcuter Ltd ☐

(c) Which ONE of the following options shows the amount in figures as it should be written on the cheque?

£333.55 ☐

£323.55 ☐

£302.55 ☐

(d) Indicate whether the following statement is true or false.

The payment terms on the invoice determines the amount of credit the customer is prepared to extend.

True ☐

False ☐

Task 9 [3 marks]

Last year your organisation recorded income and expenditure as shown in the table below:

Income and expenses	£
Sales	1,000,000
Goods for resale	450,000
Payroll costs	250,000
Electricity	20,000
Distribution costs	10,000

(a) Use the income and expenses figures to complete the following calculations:

(i) Calculate profit.

£ ☐

(ii) Calculate expenses as a percentage of sales to the nearest percentage point.

£ ☐

(b) Electricity costs for each of the previous two months were £26,000 and £19,000.

Calculate the mean monthly electricity cost for the last quarter to the nearest pound.

£ [ ]

Task 10 [2 marks]

An organisation is reviewing the selling price of some of its products.

The current selling price of product number 598 is £36.80. This is to be increased by $\frac{1}{4}$.

(a) Calculate the increase in selling price for product number 598.

£ [ ]

The current selling price of product number 396 is £21.00. This is to be increased by 7%.

(b) **Calculate the increase in selling price for product number 396.**

£ [ ]

Task 11 [5 marks]

Sales at Artim's Bakery for the last six months are as follows:

	Jul	Aug	Sept	Oct	Nov	Dec
	£	£	£	£	£	£
Sales	4,446	3,209	4,599	2,990	2,766	8,846

(a) Complete the table below to record the monthly sales figures in ascending order.

Month						
	£	£	£	£	£	£
Sales						

(b) Establish the range for monthly sales.

£ [ ]

(c) Calculate the mean monthly sales.

£ [ ]

(d) Management are targeting increasing average monthly sales by 1/3 for the next six months.

Express the target increase as a percentage to two decimal places.

[ ] %

(e) **State the ratio between sales achieved for the last six months and sales that would be achieved in the next six months if the monthly sales target is achieved.**

[ ]

Task 12 [3 marks]

Complete the following sentences by selecting the most appropriate option from the list of items below each sentence.

(a) The Fire Service is a [ ] organisation.

- private sector
- public sector
- charitable
- retail sector

(b) A limited company in the private sector [ ] aim to make a profit.

- does
- does not

(c) A bank is an example of a business in the [ ] sector.

- retail
- public
- manufacturing
- services

Task 13 [2 marks]

Indicate whether the following statements are true or false.

(a) Information provided by the finance department is used by managers within the organisation to make poorer business decisions.

True [ ]

False [ ]

(b) The ICT department provides services to other departments of an organisation.

True ☐

False ☐

Task 14 **[4 marks]**

You wish to apply for a job advertised by ABC Chemicals and have been asked to complete and send an application form.

(a) Using the items provided, complete the application form.

Full name	**Sharon Wu**
Age	**19**
Contact details	**32 First Street** **Newport** **NW2 7SE** **Mobile: 0988 234111**
Qualifications	
Experience	
Interests	

AAT Award in Business Skills

Sharonwu13@umail.com

Keen runner completed first marathon in 2016

GCSEs June 20X4 Maths – B English – C Physics – C Chemistry – B

Work experience placement as accounts clerk with Boyle's Chemists from 1 August – 30 November 2017.

Playing the piano. Currently studying for grade 8.

(b) The advertisement stated that the successful applicant must have experience of working in an accounts department.

Complete the following sentence by selecting the most appropriate option from the list of items below.

This is best described as [ ] job requirement.

Options:

a vocational
an essential
a desirable

(c) Which of the following would be the best choice to look for job opportunity if you require advice and assistance to find an appropriate vacancy?

Newspapers	☐
Recruitment agencies	☐
Recruitment websites	☐

Task 15 [3 marks]

(a) Show whether the following statements are true or false.

It is more important that documents related to sales are completed quickly than worrying about whether they are completely accurate.

True	☐
False	☐

The details describing the goods on a delivery note and related goods received note would normally be expected to match.

True	☐
False	☐

(b) You have been asked to provide to your manager a record of the amounts of all invoices sent each month, including totals for each customer and weekly totals.

Which of the following would be the most appropriate way to communicate this information?

Instant message ☐

Face-to-face ☐

Spreadsheet ☐

Task 16 [2 marks]

Complete the following sentences by inserting the most appropriate option from the list below each sentence.

Information about staff bonuses held on the computer should be kept

☐

- in an area to which all employees have access.
- in a password-protected file with access restricted to those who need the information.

A friend is a supplier of the organisation where you work. She asks you how much profit your organisation is making on items sold on. You reply:

☐

- 'I am sorry but I cannot give you any information as it is confidential.'
- 'As you are a supplier I can tell you that we add 25%.'

Task 17 [4 marks]

You work as a clerk in the finance department of Larsons Office Cleaning Ltd.

(a) **Which of the following describes the sector that Larsons operates in?**

Retailing ☐

Services ☐

Public sector ☐

The number of complaints for the first 10 days of June are as follows:

Date	1	2	3	4	5	6	7	8	9	10
Complaints	2	0	1	1	3	0	2	2	4	0

(b) State the mode for the number of daily complaints received:

[ ]

(c) State the range for the number of compliants per day:

[ ]

(d) Calculate the percentage of total complaints made represented by the highest value. Provide your answer to two decimal places.

[ ] %

Task 18 [4 marks]

HRD Electricals has received the following invoice.

INVOICE	**Invoice number 56314**		
Best Components Ltd **Unit 13,** **New Industrial Park** **Port Town PT2 3FD** **Tel: 0178 2449888**			
VAT registration:	0123 2888 36		
Date/tax point:	5 December 20XX		
Order number:	02989		
Customer:	HRD Electricals 347 High Street Lakewood LW1 7GG		
Account number (customer code)	3422 H		
Description/product code	**Quantity**	**Unit amount £**	**Total £**
LED displays	100	150.00	15,000.00
A7 Chipsets	200	42.50	8,500.00
USB ports	350	1.75	6,125 00
Net total			29,625.00
VAT at 20%			5,925.00
Invoice total			35,550.00
Terms 30 days			

(a) State the correct invoice total:

£ ☐

(b) Which of the following could have been used by Best Components as a source in preparing the invoice?

Goods received note ☐

Customer order ☐

Approved supplier list ☐

(c) HRD Electrical prepares the goods received note below when the goods are received:

GOODS RECEIVED NOTE						
Delivery from: **Best Components Ltd Unit 13, New Industrial Park Port Town PT2 3FD**			**GRN Number:**		**00444**	
			Supplier code:		**2398**	
			Order no:		**02989**	
		Date received:	**7 December 20XX**			
Account number (customer code)			**3422 H**			
Order no.	**Desc.**	**Unit price**	**Units**	**Total Price (net)**	**VAT**	**Total Price (Gross)**
32011	LED display	150.00	80	12,000.00	2,400.00	14,400.00
32011	A7 Chipset	42.50	200	8,500.00	1,700.00	10,200.00
32011	USB ports	1.75	350	612.50	122.50	735.00
Total			630	24,112.50	4,222.50	25,335.00
Received by: Martin Rigby						

Which of the following is true of the goods delivered?

Correct amount, but wrong description	☐
Correct amount and right description	☐
Incorrect amount and wrong description	☐
Incorrect amount, but right description	☐

(d) **Indicate whether the following statements are true or false.**

	True	False
Sales with payment terms of 30 days will lead to a lower bank balance for Best Components Ltd than cash sales.	☐	☐
The invoice would be sent by Best Components Ltd only after it receives the goods received note from HRD Electricals.	☐	☐

Task 19 [3 marks]

Patel's Foodmarket has the following for March 20XY:

	£
Cash sales	14,569
Credit sales	4,552
Goods for resale	8,544
Payroll costs	7,208
Other expenses	3,455

(a) Calculate the profit or loss for Patel's Foodmarket in March.

£ [ ]

(b) Patel's Foodmarket pays suppliers for goods for resale 60 days after invoice date. Payment terms for credit sales are also 60 days. Payroll costs and other expenses are paid in the month.

Calculate the change in Patel's Foodmarket's bank balance as a result of March trading?

£ [ ]

(c) Which of the following would have led to a higher monthly bank balance?

A lower proportion of total sales made on credit	☐
A higher proportion of payroll costs in total expenses	☐
A change in supplier payment terms to by end of invoice month	☐

BPP practice assessment 1: answers

Task 1 [3 marks]

(a) Losses do not affect a business's bank account. ✓

(b)

Item	Income	Expenses
Insurance		✓
Cash sale	✓	
Loan interest		✓
Credit sale	✓	

(c)

Description	Term described
A transaction to sell goods when payment is made at a later date than delivery of the goods	Credit sale
A transaction to buy goods when payment is made immediately	Cash purchase

Task 2

(a) The cost of each box of paper:

£ **5.06**

(b) The purchase of the boxes of paper is a:

credit transaction

Task 3

(a) An organisation receives **a delivery note** from a supplier with goods supplied.

An organisation sends **a purchase order** to a supplier requesting that the goods specified in the document be sold to the organisation.

(b) Sales invoice ☑

(c)

	True	False
Customers include payment terms on customer orders stating when they are prepared to pay.	☐	☑
A service business such as a law firm usually refers to people using its services as customers.	☐	☑

Task 4

(a)

Name	Jana Wozniak	
Contact details	Mobile: 0988 233 5588 65 The Pastures Laketown LK23 8ED Emial: janawoz@nmail.com	☑ **(email not emial)**
Qualifications	GCSEs Maths English French Drama A levels Maths	☑ **(no grades or dates)**
Experience	ACME Office Services I worked for ACME for 14 months from January 20X6 to March 20X7 as an accounts assistant. I left as I found it really boring and didn't pay enough.	☑ **(not professional)**

(b)

	True	False
You would not be expected to pay when using a recruitment agency to find a job.	✓	
The successful applicant for a job must meet all essential requirements.		✓

Task 5

(a) **43 hours and 45 minutes**

(b) Challenging but achievable ✓

(c) Human resources ✓

Task 6

In the accounting system, sales invoices must be entered into the accounting records individually.

(a) Information and data security ✓

(b) J@ma1 ✓

(c) Introduce back-up procedures ✓

Task 7

(a) £ **273**

(b) **7.33** %

(c) **20:1**

Task 8

(a) 24 April 20XX ✓

(b) Woodcutter Ltd ✓

(c) £323.55 ✓

(d) The payments terms on the invoice determines the amount of credit the customer is prepared to extend

False ✓

Task 9

(a)

(i) Profit

£ **270,000**

(ii) Expenses as a percentage of sales

73 %

(b) Mean electricity cost

£ **21,667**

Task 10

(a) The increase in selling price for product number 598:

£ **9.20**

(b) The increase in selling price for product number 396:

£ **1.47**

Task 11

(a)

	Nov	Oct	Aug	Jul	Sept	Dec
	£	£	£	£	£	£
Sales	2,766	2,990	3,209	4,446	4,599	8,846

(b) Range for monthly sales:

£ **6,080**

(c) Mean monthly sales:

£ **4,476**

(d) Target increase as a percentage to two decimal places:

33.33 %

(e) Ratio between sales achieved for the last six months and sales that would be achieved in the next six months if the monthly sales target is achieved:

3:4

Task 12

(a) The Fire Service is a **public sector** organisation.

(b) A limited company in the private sector **does** aim to make a profit.

(c) A bank is an example of a business in the **services** sector.

Task 13

(a) Information provided by the finance department is used by managers within the organisation to make poorer business decisions.

False ✓

(b) The ICT department provides services to other departments of an organisation.

True ✓

Task 14

(a)

Full name	**Sharon Wu**
Age	**19**
Contact details	**32 First Street** **Newport** **NW2 7SE** **Mobile: 0988 234111** Sharonwu13@umail.com
Qualifications	GCSEs June 20X4 Maths – B English – C Physics – C Chemistry – B AAT Award in Business Skills
Experience	Work experience placement as accounts clerk with Boyle's Chemists from 1 August – 30 November 2017.
Interests	Keen runner completed first marathon in 2016. Playing the piano. Currently studying for grade 8.

(b) This is best described as **essential** job requirement

(c) Recruitment agencies ✓

Task 15

(a) It is more important that documents related to sales are completed quickly than worrying about whether they are completely accurate.

False ✓

The details describing goods on a delivery note and related goods received note would normally be expected to match.

True ✓

(b) Spreadsheet ✓

Task 16

Information about staff bonuses held on the computer should be kept:

in a password-protected file with access restricted to those who need the information.

A friend is a supplier of the organisation where you work. She asks you how much profit your organisation is making on items sold on. You reply:

'I am sorry but I cannot give you any information as it is confidential.'

Task 17

(a) Services ✓

(b) 2

(c) 4

(d) 26.67 %

Task 18

(a) £ **28,935**

(b) Customer order ✓

(c) Incorrect amount, but right description ✓

(d)

	True	False
Sales with payment terms of 30 days will lead to a lower bank balance for Best Components Ltd than cash sales.	✓	
The invoice would be sent by Best Components Ltd only after it receives the goods received note from HRD Electricals	✓	

Task 19

(a) £ **(86)**

(b) £ **3,906**

(c) A lower proportion total sales made on credit ✓

BPP practice assessment 2

Task 1 [2 marks]

Organisations have assets, liabilities, income and expenditure.

(a) Which ONE of the following statements is true?

Expenses are something an organisation sells. ☐

Customer invoices show the amount of expenses. ☐

Income is generated by credit sales. ☐

(b) Place a tick in the appropriate column of the table below to show whether each of the items listed is an example of an income or expenditure. You should not place more than one tick (✓) against each item.

Item	Income	Expenses
Bank interest received		
Goods purchased for resale		
Sales paid for immediately		
Sales paid 10 days after invoice date		

Task 2 [2 marks]

You work for Acme Trading as a purchase order clerk. You have been asked to place an order for 14 office chairs.

(a) What would be the best procedure for finding a supplier?

Ask a friend to recommend a supplier ☐

Use Acme Trading's approved supplier list ☐

Use an internet search engine ☐

(b) Your chosen supplier, Standard Furniture Ltd has a price before VAT of £75 per chair. Acme Trading has arranged a 15% discount with Standard Furniture.

Calculate the amount Acme Trading should be invoiced by Standard Trading including VAT.

£ [ ]

Task 3 [3 marks]

Your organisation sold 8 desks on 27 August for £240.40 in total to JP Fitters Company.

(a) What is the price of each desk?

£ [ ]

Your organisation issued an invoice asking JP Fitters Company to pay for the desks within 30 days.

(b) Is the sale of the desks a cash transaction or a credit transaction?

[ ]

(c) Total sales for 27 August are £1,200.

Which one of the following fractions most closely describes the of sale to JP Fitters as a proportion of the total sales for the day?

1/4 ☐

1/5 ☐

1/10 ☐

Task 4 [3 marks]

Complete the following sentences by selecting the most appropriate option from the list below.

An organisation sends [ ] to a customer listing goods sold to the customer and showing the amount due to be paid, and when it is due to be paid.

An organisation provides [ ] to a customer when it supplies goods ordered.

An organisation receives [ ] from a customer requesting that the goods specified in the document be sold to the customer.

List of terms

a purchase order
a delivery note
a goods received note
an invoice

Task 5 [4 marks]

The monthly payroll costs for Smyth Traders for the last quarter are as follows: January – twelve thousand, four hundred and fifty three pounds; February – eleven thousand, four hundred and thirty two pounds; March – thirteen thousand, four hundred and one pounds.

(a) **Record sales as figures ranking them in ascending order.**

Month			
	£	£	£
Payroll costs			

(b) **Calculate mean monthly payroll costs for the quarter to the nearest pound.**

£ [ ]

(c) **If payroll costs for the quarter make up 28% of total expenses, what level of sales must Smyth Traders achieve in order to break even for the quarter? Provide your answer to the nearest pound.**

£ [ ]

(d) **Using the information for the last quarter, estimate Smyth Traders' payroll costs for the year to the nearest pound.**

£ [ ]

Task 6 [3 marks]

You wish to apply for the following job.

> **Company: KwikClik Ltd**
>
> **Position offered: Accounts clerk**
>
> This is an opportunity to join the finance function of a rapidly growing internet retailer based in Rivertown. Applicants must have experience of data entry into a computerised accounting system and have worked in a finance department for at least one year. The ability to work under pressure with a high degree of accuracy is essential.
>
> Preference will be given to candidates who have an accounting qualification or who have a high level of competence in the use of spreadsheet software. The successful candidate is likely to have experience of working in a retail environment.
>
> A competitive salary and benefits package is offered depending on experience.
>
> Please contact Marita Jones on 0207 9977222 for an application form. Closing date for postal applications 31 March 20XX.

(a) Which of the following is not essential to be considered for this position?

Data entry experience	☐
Ability to work under pressure	☐
Retail experience	☐
Finance department work experience	☐

(b) Which of the following is likely to be the least important for a person applying for this job?

Good level of numeracy	☐
Strong selling skills	☐
Attention to detail	☐
Ability to use spreadsheets	☐

(c) Which of the following would be an appropriate action to get the job?

Send a CV to KwikClik on 2 April	☐
Send a completed application form to KwikClik on 25 March	☐
Send a CV to KwikClik on 25 March	☐
Send a completed application form to KwikClik on 2 April	☐

Task 7 [4 marks]

You work for J & M Hardware in the finance team and you have been asked to urgently raise and send a purchase order for a purchase of three office computers. There are three computer suppliers on J & M Hardware's approved supplier list. Each has a different list price and each reduces the price it charges J & M by a different trade discount.

(a) Using the information below select the lowest-cost supplier.

Supplier	List price	Discount	Select (✓)
Barry Computers	854	20%	
Colwyn Electronics	795	12%	
Swansea Technology	810	15%	

(b) Complete the following sentence.

The trade discount offered by Barry computers means that the price paid by J & M will be ☐ lower than their list prices.

Options:

1/4
1/5
1/10
1/20

(c) Which of the following would be sent by J & M Hardware to the selected supplier in the course of the transaction?

Delivery note ☐

Purchase order ☐

Goods received note ☐

Purchase invoice ☐

(d) You had previously been given permission to leave early today to attend a medical appointment but you have not finished raising the invoice for the computer purchase. If you leave the urgent order for the computers will not be completed.

Which ONE of the following actions should you NOT take?

Tell your supervisor that you haven't completed the invoice so that the tasks can be completed by a colleague. ☐

Record of the work you have done on the purchase so far, and list the outstanding work, so that another team members can follow what you have done. ☐

Cancel your medical appointment. ☐

Task 8 [3 marks]

You are employed in the finance department of Cheepo Supermarkets.

(a) Complete the following sentence.

The organisation you work for [ ] to make a profit and is part of the [ ] sector.

Options:

aims
does not aim
manufacturing
services
retail

(b) Which of the following is most likely to correctly describe Cheepo Supermarkets?

A limited company ☐

A charity ☐

A public sector organisation ☐

(c) Cheepo Supermarkets wishes to recruit an individual to work in customer service dealing with customer complaints and queries face-to-face.

Which one of the following attributes is least likely to be an essential requirement for the job?

Strong interpersonal skills ☐

A high level of numeracy ☐

Smart appearance ☐

Task 9 [4 marks]

On 14 April 20XY you are preparing an invoice for five hundred and forty-five pounds and two pence to send to a customer, Easy Easels in relation to goods supplied.

(a) Which ONE of the following options shows the date as it should be written on the invoice?

14.5.XY ☐

14 April 20XY ☐

4.14.20XY ☐

(b) Which ONE of the following options shows the payee as it should be written on the invoice?

Easy's ☐

Easels ☐

Easy Easels ☐

(c) Which ONE of the following options shows the amount in figures as it should be shown on the invoice?

£545.02 ☐

£545.20 ☐

£500.45 ☐

(d) Indicate whether the following statement is true or false.

The date on the invoice should be the day the customer order was received.

True ☐

False ☐

Task 10 [3 marks]

At the end of every year the business you work for calculates the profit or loss for the year.

(a) Indicate whether the following statement is true or false.

If income exceeds expenditure, the organisation has made a loss.

True ☐

False ☐

Last year your organisation recorded income and expenditure as shown in the table below:

Income and expenditure	£
Sales	890,000
Goods for resale	653,780
Labour	124,740
Administration	45,700
Delivery costs	800

(b) Use the income and expenditure figures to complete the following calculations:

(i) Calculate profit.

£ [ ]

(ii) Calculate profit as a percentage of sales. Show your answer to the nearest whole percentage point.

[ ] %

(c) Show the proportion of sales required to cover expenses as a decimal. Provide your answer to two decimal places.

[ ]

Task 11 [2 marks]

An organisation is reviewing the selling price of some of its products.

The current selling price of product number 59 is £16.60. This is to be increased by $\frac{1}{4}$ (one quarter).

(a) Calculate the increase in selling price for product number 59.

£ [ ]

The current selling price of product number 36 is £8.50. This is to be increased by 2%.

(b) Calculate the increase in selling price for product number 36.

£ [ ]

Task 12 [4 marks]

Your organisation keeps detailed records of costs.

Repair costs for each of four production machines are shown in the table below.

(a) Complete the table below to show the repair costs for Machine 1.

	£
Machine 1	[ ]
Machine 2	208.12
Machine 3	345.77
Machine 4	105.11
Total	816.20

(b) Calculate the mean average service and repair cost per machine.

£ [ ]

Costs relating to Factory 1 are shown in the table below.

(c) Complete the table to show the total costs relating to Factory 1.

Item	£
Electricity	1,200.50
Wages	3,450.20
Security	51.15
Insurance	153.45
Total costs	

(d) Which of the following is the ratio of the cost of insurance to the cost of security?

Options:

3:1
4:1
5:1

Task 13 [3 marks]

Complete the following sentences by selecting the most appropriate option from the list of items below each sentence.

(a) A partnership is a [ ] organisation.

- private sector
- public sector
- charitable

(b) A sole trader [ ] aim to make a profit.

- does
- does not

(c) Which of the following departments would a services sector business NOT be expected to have?

Finance	☐
Human Resource	☐
ICT	☐
Production	☐

Task 14 **[5 marks]**

You work as a finance clerk for Nowak Ltd. The company has two factories producing the same component for the automotive industry. One is in Newbridge and the other is in Oldchester.

(a) A summary of the number of units has been produced by a colleague for each of the last four weeks.

Identify and correct any errors in the shaded areas.

Week	Oldchester	Newbridge	Total
1	2,564	1,230	3,794
2	2,650	956	3,606
3	1,988	859	2,874
4	2,209	1,110	3,319
4	2,209	1,110	3,319
Total	9,411	3,155	12,566

(b) Calculate to two decimal places the mean number or units produced by the Oldchester factory per week.

☐ **units**

(c) Assuming that both factories operate seven days a week, estimate how long it will take the Oldchester factory to produce 5,000 units to the nearest whole day?

☐ **days**

(d) Calculate to two decimal places the percentage of total number of units produced in week 4 made by the Newbridge factory.

☐ **%**

(e) **Which of the following best describes the sector that Nowak Ltd operates in?**

Services ☐

Manufacturing ☐

Retail ☐

Task 15 [5 marks]

You work for MK Manufacturing and have been asked to send an email to Chris Cairns, the production manager, confirming the number of parts of XY that have been purchased in the year to date.

Using the items on the next page, compose an appropriate email in the template below.

You will not need to use all of the items.

From: AATstudent@MKM.com **To:** **Subject:**

chriscairns@MKM.com	XY parts
Purchases of XY parts year to date	Hi Mate
Please could you confirm the total number of XY parts that have been purchased in the year to date?	Kind regards AAT student
chrischairns@MKM.com	Hi Chris
How many XY parts have you bought this year?	Cheers AAT student

Task 16 [2 marks]

(a) Indicate whether the following statements are true or false.

Organisations use standardised procedures and documents for sales and purchases to improve efficiency and save time.

True ☐

False ☐

The format of documents for sales and purchases is set out by law.

True ☐

False ☐

You have been asked to send an application pack to someone enquiring after a job in your organisation.

(b) Select the most appropriate form of communication to accompany the application pack.

☐ Letter

☐ Spreadsheeet

☐ Report

Task 17 [5 marks]

It is important to observe confidentiality.

Complete the following sentences by inserting the most appropriate option from the list below each sentence.

Chandra is working on the payroll. She leaves her desk to make a cup of tea. She should:

- leave the payroll documents on her desk, as she'll only be gone five minutes.
- lock the payroll documents in her desk drawer, because she will be away from her desk.

A friend is a journalist, writing a story on local businesses for the local paper. She asks you how many people your organisation employs. You reply:

- '200.'
- 'I don't think it is appropriate for you to ask me; you should contact the managing director.'

Task 18 [2 marks]

(a) Indicate which of the following would be the best place to identify a job opportunity which incorporates a significant element of training.

Recruitment agencies	☐
Newspapers	☐
Apprenticeship providers	☐

(b) Which of the following would be the best approach once you have prepared your CV?

Send it as soon as possible without checking	☐
Carefully check it yourself	☐
Carefully check it yourself twice	☐
Carefully check it yourself, then get another person to check it	☐

Task 19 [2 marks]

Add arrows to the diagram to show the documents sent to suppliers and customers by XYZ Ltd as part of its procedures related to sales and purchases. Not all the arrows provided will be required.

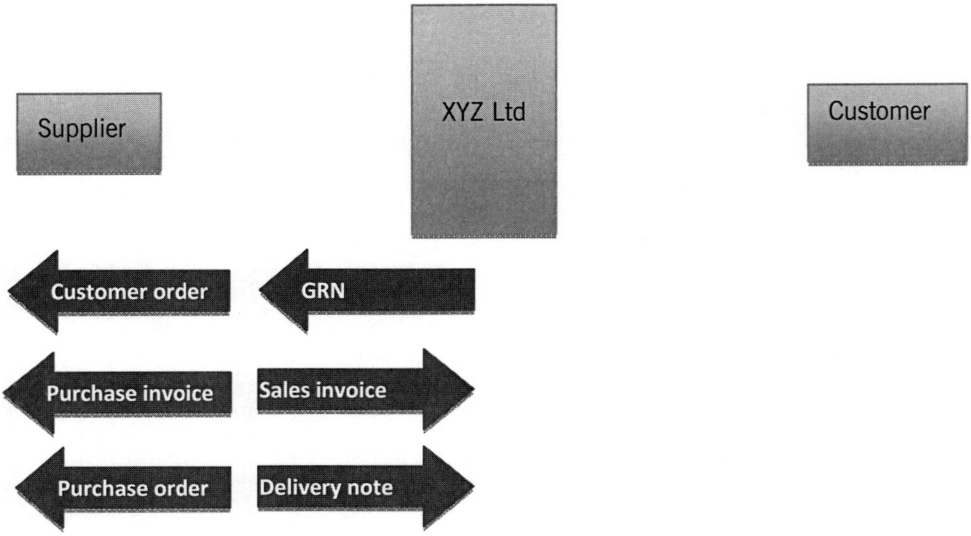

Task 20 [2 marks]

(a) Complete this sentence by inserting the most appropriate option from the list next to each box.

An employee in the finance department should [ ]

and be [ ]

be punctual	polite at all times.
be practical	polite unless irritated.

(b) Indicate whether the following statements are true or false.

Regular use of social media to communicate with friends while at work is acceptable because it will not disturb co-workers.

True ☐

False ☐

The person who sets your goals at work and monitors your performance is determined by the organisation's reporting lines.

True ☐

False ☐

BPP practice assessment 2: answers

Task 1

(a) Income is generated by credit sales. ☑

(b)

Item	Income	Expenses
Bank interest received	✓	
Goods purchased for resale		✓
Sales paid for immediately	✓	
Sales paid 10 days after invoice date	✓	

Task 2

(a) Use Acme Trading's approved supplier list ☑

(b)

£ **1,071**

Working: Gross price 14 × 75 × 120% = 1,260
Less discount 1,260 × 15% = (189)
1,071

Task 3

(a) The price of each desk is:

£ **30.05**

(b) The sale is a:

credit transaction

(c) 1/5 ☑

Task 4

An organisation sends **an invoice** to a customer listing goods sold to the customer and showing the amount due to be paid, and when it is due to be paid.

An organisation provides **a delivery note** to a customer when it supplies goods ordered.

An organisation receives **a purchase order** from a customer requesting that the goods specified in the document be sold to the customer.

Task 5

(a) ✓

Month	February	January	March
	£	£	£
Payroll costs	11,432	12,453	13,401

(b) £ **12,429**

(c) £ **133,164**

Working: (11,432 +12,453 +13,401) ÷ 0.28 = 133,164

(d) £ **149,144**

Working: (11,432 +12,453 +13,401) × 4

Task 6

(a) Retail experience ✓

(b) Strong selling skills ✓

(c) Send a completed application form to KwikClik on 25 March ✓

Task 7

(a)

Supplier	List price	Discount	Select (✓)
Barry Computers	854	20%	✓
Colwyn Electronics	795	12%	
Swansea Technology	810	15%	

(b) The trade discount offered by Barry computers means that the price paid by J & M will be **1/5** lower than their list prices.

(c) Purchase order ✓

(d) The most appropriate option is:

Cancel your medical appointment. ✓

This question makes clear that you are working as part of a team so the other two options are reasonable responses to not completing an urgent task. It is not in your company's interest for you not to attend a medical appointment.

Task 8

(a) The organisation you work for **aims** to make a profit and is part of the **retail** sector.

(b) A limited company ✓

(c) A high level of numeracy ✓

Task 9

(a) 14 April 20XY ✓

(b) Easy Easels ✓

(c) £545.02 ✓

(d) False ✓

The date on the invoice would not pre-date the supply of goods.

Task 10

(a) False ✓

(b) **(i)** Profit

£ **64,980**

(ii) Profit as a percentage of sales

7 %

(c) Proportion of sales required to cover expenses

0.93

Task 11

(a) The increase in selling price for product number 59:

£ **4.15**

(b) The increase in selling price for product number 36:

£ **0.17**

Task 12

(a) Repair costs for Machine 1

	£
Machine 1	**157.20**
Machine 2	208.12
Machine 3	345.77
Machine 4	105.11
Total	816.20

(b) The average service and repair cost per machine

£ **204.05**

(c) Total key costs relating to Factory 1

Item	£
Electricity	1,200.50
Wages	3,450.20
Security	51.15
Insurance	153.45
Total key costs	**4,855.30**

(d) The ratio of the cost of insurance to the cost of security

3:1

Task 13

(a) A partnership is a **private sector** organisation.

(b) A sole trader **does** aim to make a profit.

(c) Production ✓

Task 14

(a)

Week	Oldchester	Newbridge	Total
1	2,564	1,230	3,794
2	2,650	956	3,606
3	1,988	859	**2,847**
4	2,209	1,110	3,319
Total	9,411	**4,155**	**13,556**

(b) **6,507.75** units

(c) **15** **days**

Working: Average daily output 9411 ÷ 28 = 336

5000 ÷ 336 = 14.88 = 15 days

(d) **33.44** **%**

(e) Manufacturing ✓

Task 15

From:	**AATstudent@MKM.com**
To:	**chriscairns@MKM.com**
Subject:	**Purchases of XY parts year to date**

Hi Chris

Please could you confirm the total number of XY parts that have been purchased in the year to date.

Kind regards
AAT student

Task 16

(a) Organisations use standardised procedures and documents for sales and purchases to improve efficiency and save time.

True ☑

The format of documents for sales and purchases is set out by law.

False ☑

(b) The most appropriate form of communication to accompany the application pack is:

☑ Letter

Task 17

Chandra is working on the payroll. She leaves her desk to make a cup of tea. She should:

lock the payroll documents in her desk drawer because she will be away from her desk.

A friend is a journalist, writing a story on local businesses for the local paper. She asks you how many people your organisation employs. You reply:

'I don't think it is appropriate for you to ask me; you should request a meeting with the managing director.'

Task 18

(a) Apprenticeship providers ☑

(b) Carefully check it yourself, then get another person to check it ☑

Task 19

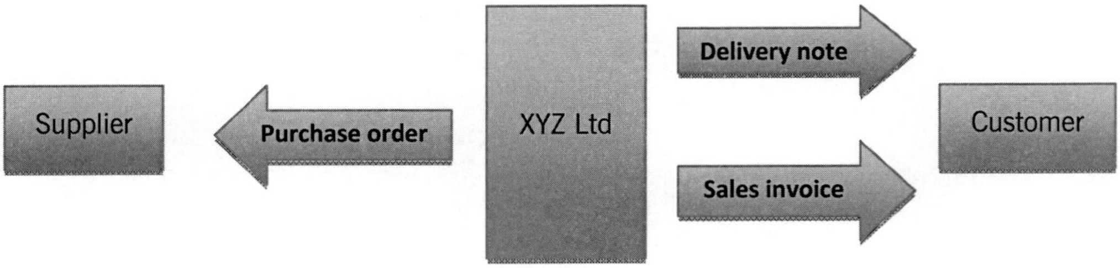

Task 20

(a) An employee in the finance department should **be punctual** and be **polite at all times.**

(b) Regular use of social media to communicate with friends while at work is acceptable because it will not disturb co-workers.

False ✓

The person who sets your goals at work and monitors your performance is determined by the organisation's reporting lines.

True ✓

Index

REVIEW FORM

How have you used this Workbook?
(Tick one box only)

☐ Home study

☐ On a course ____________________

☐ Other ____________________

Why did you decide to purchase this Workbook? *(Tick one box only)*

☐ Have used BPP Workbooks in the past

☐ Recommendation by friend/colleague

☐ Recommendation by a college lecturer

☐ Saw advertising

☐ Other ____________________

During the past six months do you recall seeing/receiving either of the following?
(Tick as many boxes as are relevant)

☐ Our advertisement in *Accounting Technician*

☐ Our Publishing Catalogue

Which (if any) aspects of our advertising do you think are useful?
(Tick as many boxes as are relevant)

☐ Prices and publication dates of new editions

☐ Information on Workbook content

☐ Details of our free online offering

☐ None of the above

Your ratings, comments and suggestions would be appreciated on the following areas of this Workbook.

	Very useful	*Useful*	*Not useful*
Introduction	☐	☐	☐
Quality of explanations	☐	☐	☐
How it works	☐	☐	☐
Chapter tasks	☐	☐	☐
Chapter Overviews	☐	☐	☐
Test your learning	☐	☐	☐
Keywords	☐	☐	☐
BPP practice assessments	☐	☐	☐
Index	☐	☐	☐

	Excellent	*Good*	*Adequate*	*Poor*
Overall opinion of this Workbook	☐	☐	☐	☐

Do you intend to continue using BPP Products? ☐ Yes ☐ No

Please note any further comments and suggestions/errors on the reverse of this page.
The BPP author of this edition can be emailed at: lmfeedback@bpp.com.

Alternatively, the Head of Programme of this edition can be emailed at: nisarahmed@bpp.com.

REVIEW FORM (continued)

TELL US WHAT YOU THINK

Please note any further comments and suggestions/errors below.